# Spitting Fire

## Your Guide to Reignite and Maintain Your Passion at Home, Work and Beyond

*By Lauren LeMunyan*

D1166730

LLC, LLC

Washington, DC, USA

Published 2018

## DISCLAIMER

Cover Design: Lauren LeMunyan

Front Cover and Back Cover Photo: Debra Alfarone

Editing: Jennifer Burgess, Colleen Forsyth and Tom Johnson

*To Grandma (Dolly)*

Thank you for teaching me skills that continue

to weave opportunities in my life.


*To Mom*

We're not small. We're highly concentrated.

Thank you for being my ultimate reframer!

# Table of Contents

# Intro

## My Hopes For You, The Reader

I am so pumped that you chose this book over the thousands of other ways you could be spending your time. This book has been in the making for three years. Well, 34 years, really. This is my third attempt at writing a book, but it's the first time that I knew my message was ready to publish and share with the world.

So who am I, and what business do I have writing this kind of book?

I'm not a celebrity. I'm not an Instagram influencer with 100,000 followers. I'm not a public figure. (No blue check on Twitter yet.) I'm just like you, dealing with the ups and downs of being a thirtysomething business owner. When stretched outside my comfort zone, I experience self-doubt, second-guessing, and self-sabotage. Some days, I want to stay in bed and shut out the world. And there are times when I want to throw in the towel and give up. I'm human.

I wanted to write this book to share the lessons I've learned from becoming a certified coach, running a full-time business, and learning from my amazing clients. I want to give you tools that you can apply to your own journey of SpitFire awesomeness.

This book is not a silver bullet for success. I don't expect you to read it and have your whole life figured out. I just want you to add it as another resource in your journey to living an awesome life.

Here are my hopes for you after you read this book:

1.  You'll be more connected to your power and passion.
2.  You'll carry a permission slip in your back pocket that allows you to take those scary steps into the unknown.
3.  You'll feel the fire in your belly and know when it's time to use it.
4.  You'll own and enforce your boundaries.
5.  You'll be better able to identify the things that suck away your energy and make you stumble.
6.  You'll have a Self-Care strategy for managing your energy buildups and declines.
7.  You'll feel the connection of fellow SpitFires all around you.
8.  You'll tap into your community of fellow powerhouses.
9.  You'll unapologetically be yourself.
10. You'll own your new title: SpitFire.

Take your time with this book. Reflect. Journal. Discuss. No one expects you to figure everything out overnight. During a time of silent reflection, you may have a moment of clarity, when concepts and experiences start clicking together.

Here's my big tip for getting the most out of this book: Be patient. Have patience with this book, with its contents, and most importantly, with you.

# Chapter 1

## The Story of The SpitFire Coach

We're going to be diving into all things **you**, so I thought it would only be fair for you to know a little more about me. As I learned while attempting to write book #2, it's better to share your overall story, not your super-secret diary. I'll be sharing the highlights of my journey to becoming The SpitFire Coach.

My name is Lauren LeMunyan, The JRSY FRSH rapper, Facilitator of Awesomeness, and The SpitFire Coach. Yes, all those titles are self-designated, but when you own your company, you can call yourself whatever you want.

So how did I get to be a Rapping, Awesomeness-Facilitating, Fire-Spitting Strategic Business and Life Coach? Here's my story...

## Crocheting, Passion, and Entrepreneurship

The first time I heard the term "SpitFire," I was six or seven years old. With young divorced parents, my grandparents became the economically friendly option for childcare during holidays, summers, and long weekends in upstate New York.

As the oldest sister of eight, my grandma was the matriarch of her family. Most of her siblings lived within twenty minutes of one another, and the house was always buzzing with visitors or we frequently popped over for visits. Whether it was a wedding, christening, or funeral, a family event always seemed to be going on when we visited. (Don't worry, I'm getting to the SpitFire part.)

At six years old, I decided that I wanted to learn to crochet, after realizing that the cookies and lemonade options were much better at my grandma's Tuesday Night Crochet Club. So I asked my grandma to teach me how to crochet an afghan, and her eyes glowed with pride.

When I grew frustrated by the uneven stitches, she reminded me to "be patient." I would spend hours creating chains (the base stitches of crochet), then present them to her for approval before learning the next stitch. She would quickly pinpoint the inconsistencies and unravel all my hard work. My heart sank, but I knew I had to try again—to make it to the next level and start creating presentable items. After a few weeks, I was on crochet cruise control!

One summer afternoon shortly thereafter, my Great Uncle Eddie and Aunt Alice were hosting one of our many summertime family get-togethers in New Windsor, NY. I proudly hauled my yarn and hooks into their house, and tucked my latest project next to the couch, to keep them away from the chaos of familial foot traffic.

A slew of second and third cousins ran through the house before they were shooed outside. I joined them for a round of tag, but after the boys started transitioning into roughhousing, I strategized my return to my home base: the sofa. That was my safety zone.

When I picked up my favorite red-I hook, I felt a surge of energy run through me. Without looking down, my hands started cranking, with my signature right-index finger sticking out. I was entrenched in every centimeter of progress that emerged from my bag of yarn. I was in a creative trance. Then I heard it: "She's a little SpitFire. Look at her go!" I paused and wondered what that meant, but didn't ask, for fear of breaking my rhythm.

I look back on that day as my SpitFire spark, but my grandma was the true catalyst. She didn't let me slide on subpar stitches, and didn't let me leave the dinner table before my plate was clear. She was rock-solid and tough, but also soft and generous.

My grandma singlehandedly held our family together. When someone was sick, she was there dropping off food, taking care of children, and bringing in newspapers. She even maintained a regular phone tree, in order to check in on everyone in the neighborhood. Grandma didn't mess around.  So how do crocheting and my grandma connect to my SpitFire story?

On and off throughout my preteen years, I picked up simple crochet patterns from my grandma. My favorite was the "Granny Square," which could be combined to make patterns and doilies.

In junior high, it wasn't considered cool to take on the octogenarian arts, so I tabled my hooking craft for years. But things changed for me during my junior year of high school, when I took that simple Granny Square and turned it into a hat.

I had just transferred to Solebury School, a private liberal-thinking high school. The teachers encouraged us to call them by their first names, and they wanted us to speak our minds during our weekly general assemblies. The cool-kid equation was a totally different ballgame there. People celebrated independent thinking, creativity, and individuality. I started crocheting again and realized that my makeshift hat pattern could be a desirable item.

My soccer teammates soon caught wind of my new skill and started requesting hats. I started with a couple designs and then more classmates requested hats and offered to pay. My first business was born: Happy Hats! I was whipping up a hat every 20 minutes and was making money during car rides to away games.

I took Happy Hats to college with me. Between binge-drinking and studying, I would make hats for my sorority sisters, and even had a sale to benefit the American Cancer Society. It was an awesome way to be creative and make some extra cash.

Following my mom's second divorce, I transferred to Rutgers in New Jersey. Money was tight. In addition to working as an assistant in an insurance firm and taking night classes, I crocheted at night like a machine, making anywhere from two to ten hats before my hands seized up.

After working the Central Jersey craft-fair circuit for two years, I felt like I had my finger on the pulse of twentysomething color and design. In one afternoon, I was making $200-$400, a far cry from the $10/hour jobs I was being offered as a 19-year-old. With every 20-dollar bill I earned, I notched higher on the confidence scale. And with every transaction, I inched closer from hobbyist crafter to full-fledged business owner. My side hustle was providing a nice way to support myself and pay my rent.

A friend of a friend gave me the info for a young-designer market in SoHo. I looked up the website and decided that Sunday would be the day. It cost $100 to rent a 6-ft space (table not included). I knew I needed an elevated surface, but TV trays were too heavy and small. Then my shelving caught my eye. The lightweight plastic top and removable legs would easily fit into a suitcase, and only added two pounds. I took an early train into Manhattan with two large suitcases, filled to the brim with vacuum-sealed bags of hats. From Penn Station, I'd schlep the suitcases up and down the subway stairs, until I made it to the young-designer market on Mulberry Street.

Logistically, I knew I could do it, but comparing myself to real New York designers triggered my inner critic: "Who do you think you are, playing with the big boys? You crochet. You're not a designer. You're going to get laughed out of there." All of that doubt should've made me turn back, but it didn't. My inner fire raged: "You can and must do this."

There I stood outside a 100-year-old church on Mulberry Street, ready to test my designer chops. "Here goes nothing," I thought to myself as I moved through the heavy doors into a gymnasium with fifty other aspiring designers. I was covered in sweat, even though it was January.

The market itself was centered on the basketball court, but the check-in was on the nearby stage. I walked up the stairs of the platform, where a gruff, tattooed, bald guy was sifting through papers in a bin. When I asked for a table, he looked me up and down, sizing up my courage and talent with every blink. "Hundred bucks. No refunds. No tables. Cash only." I reached into my wallet and grabbed five crumpled 20s. "Spot 12," he grumbled.

I took a deep breath. Here we go. I wheeled my wares over and started unloading my setup. My new neighbors watched me out of the corners of their eyes to see if I had anything that would compete with their stuff. My makeshift tables only came up to my knees. "Good thing I'm small," I thought to myself.

After unloading almost 100 hats, I was ready. I had handmade price tags and descriptions, and I placed the hats according to size and color. If I couldn't beat their years of experience, I would best them with charm and customer service.

Before the doors opened, all the other space-renters took a lap around the space to survey the competition. But I didn't get that memo, so I stayed put in Spot 12. Before smartphones, you couldn't aimlessly scroll and avoid eye contact, so I used my fallback zone out tactic: crocheting.

That's when I met Stella, my first designer friend in New York. She approached my table and asked, "You made all this yourself?"

"Yes, these are all mine."

"You new to this?"

"Yes, my friend told me about this place. It's my first time," I sheepishly answered.

"Okay cool. Let me know if you want to split a table next time."

"Is that allowed?" I asked.

"As long as they're getting their money, they don't care what goes in the space."

"Oh okay. I'll let you know after I see how today goes."

She nodded and returned to her table. Just then, the doors to the public opened, bringing in a gush of brisk January air. As I started slinging my hats, I was glad I had gloves with me. Tourists with bare heads flooded in, and my pockets were soon filling with 20s. As people shopped, I customized and made hats from scratch. By seeing me create hats in 20 minutes or less, I earned the respect of my neighbors and patrons. I carved my spot in that market.

As the crowd died down, I stopped by Stella's table to check out her stuff and make arrangements. I rolled my shoulders back and exhaled. "I'm in for sharing a table next week."

"Cool. Let's get a drink around the corner."

I wasn't of drinking age yet, but I was willing to take the risk to get into a new circle of friends. After packing up our stuff, we wheeled it up Mulberry and squeezed into a tiny hole-in-the-wall Irish Bar on Houston. The clientele was as rough as the tattered flooring. We found an opening at the bar, and shoved our bags in between barstools. Even though I was exhausted, I was energized about my new role as designer and business owner.

"Two double Makers. We're celebrating this SpitFire." There was that designation was again.

Now, I could end this story and tell you that I became a super-confident business owner and conquered the world without any setbacks or self-doubt, but that would be a big fat lie. And now that we're friends, our relationship should be based on honesty.

It wasn't an easy road. I was sick all the time. When I wasn't in night classes or working at the insurance firm, I was churning out crocheted hats. Every hat was currency. If I didn't produce, I couldn't make money. I essentially treated myself and my body like a factory, and didn't service my health, mind, or spirit. My hands and immune system failed me.

Then the season changed, and no one wanted hats. Suddenly, I had piles of hats in every color you can imagine. I was two months from graduating, and I had a busted seasonal business with very little savings. I didn't plan for a slowdown or cumulative expenses. My short-sighted strategy bit me in the butt and triggered my long-standing history of having a scarcity mentality.

**Side Note:** *For those of you who don't know, scarcity mentality is a belief system that enforces the idea that there's never enough to go around. So if someone else has money or an opportunity, then you won't be able to have it. In this mindset, it's challenging to be happy for another person's success, because you question what it means for you or when or if you'll ever have another opportunity.*

## Adulting (aka Burying My SpitFire Self)

The moment I realized that my hat business was over, I freaked out and cried a lot. Then I decided I needed a way to make some quick money before I graduated and moved to Washington, DC. I didn't have a job lined up, but I did have three interviews scheduled for the day after graduation. (Yes, I'm a hyper-planner, and I started reaching out to association management companies three months before I graduated.)

My then-boyfriend's dad had connections at a Hyatt Hotel, so I put away my hooks and started waiting tables at the sports bar there. I have to give service workers some serious credit. It's backbreaking work, and I only lasted eight weeks. When we were busy, I was always exhausted, but I made awesome money. When we were slow, it was mind-numbing and disheartening. While there, I learned the true arts of memorization, multitasking, and schmoozing for moola.

The day after I graduated from Rutgers, I took the first train of the day down to DC and went to my first interview at an association management company on Eye Street. I'd purchased a brand-new Tahari suit and Nine West black pumps from the outlets, and I looked like a mini mogul! I was nervous when I walked in, but I knew I had experience on my side. And I could talk about pretty much anything relevant: marketing, sales, operations, project management, and merchandising.

The first thing they mentioned was my hat business. In fact, that subject dominated most of the conversation. "My little hobby could launch me into my first salaried job. This is pretty awesome!" I thought to myself.

The next day, I had an interview in Old Town Alexandria, Virginia. I was petrified to take a bus, so I hoofed it in my heels from Glover Park to the closest metro station in Tenleytown, which was over a mile away. And it was all uphill.

After almost an hour of trekking up Wisconsin Avenue, I made it to the station. Then my phone rang. It was the CEO of ASG offering me the job. I hadn't even made it to interview #2, and I was already being offered 30k a year as an Account Administrator. I was so excited. Looking back, I can't remember if I immediately said yes, or if I called my mom first. I'm pretty sure I called my mom because that's what I ALWAYS do. During my metro ride, I accepted the position with the eager innocence of someone just starting out.

I ended up finally making it to my interview after telling them I would be super-late and that I had a job offer. By the time I arrived at their offices, I was a hot mess. I had holes in my stockings, a blister forming on my heel, and sweat everywhere.

Those ladies were so patient and gracious. We had a lovely chat before they took pity on me and dropped me off at the metro station.

*Side Note:* *When interviewing, always double the amount of time you think it will take to get there.*

As I headed back to New Jersey, I was elated and ready to give notice and move to DC. I had eight days to pack up and move— except I didn't have anywhere to live, and I didn't have a ton of money saved up. My friend put me in touch with a woman who graciously let me crash on her living room floor.

When I thought that the houseguest invitation didn't have an expiration date, my naiveté got the better of me again. In fact, it did. After two weeks, I was out on the curb with my stuff, totally distraught. I'd been looking for an apartment. But with no paycheck and limited funds, it felt impossible to find a place.

I ended up calling this guy I'd met. He gave me the creeps, but I knew I could crash at his place for a couple of nights, until I figured out my next move. But after an unwanted physical advance in the middle of the night, I knew I had to get out of there.

Thankfully, AOL Instant Messenger was alive and well, and people were awesome about updating their locations. I found another friend from college, Molly, and pinged her from work. I was upfront about my situation, and she became my lifeline. It was a Friday, and I went directly to her place from work. I didn't have all my belongings, just a backpack with necessities. For the first time in two weeks, I could breathe.

I started questioning if I'd made the right decision. Why was I in such a rush to move to DC? I was comfortable and making decent money in New Jersey. And now I was essentially homeless, and I still hadn't received my first paycheck. But I never called home and asked to return. I never gave up. Instead, I dug my heels in at work and put in extra hours. As the newest hire at a company of six, I knew in my gut that there was an opportunity for substantial advancement, if I showed them my full potential.

I stayed with Molly for three weeks, until I found a cute little (and I mean little) basement apartment back in Glover Park, where I'd first stayed when I went to the interview. It had a bus stop right outside, seven-foot ceilings, and a hot-pink bedroom. The refrigerator didn't keep anything cold, and the backyard was infested with mosquitos. But it was my own space.

At $750 a month, it quickly gobbled up my $1700 per month of take-home pay. I tucked away whatever savings I could, hoping that my income would increase at some point.

I made it work by spending as little as I could and working the dating system. I'm not proud of it, but I did what I could to stay afloat. I went on 3-5 dates a week and worked my charm to get my drinks and food paid for. That's when my drinking really picked up.

At the time, I didn't realize how much stress I was under. I had a limited support system, and no clue how to be an adult on my own. Happy Hour served as an easy way to dull out the expectations, comparisons, and judgments that filled my head when it was quiet. I wasn't happy or healthy, but I didn't know how to do anything else. I only knew how to keep pushing and hoped that things would get better.

Soon, I learned that things sometimes have to get harder before they get better. In fact, within my first 90 days of full-time employment, I experienced my first dose of sexual harassment and a dash of backlash from a female supervisor.

I loved working with the meeting planner on staff. She was patient and caring, and let me work with her on an upcoming client convention. It was the first time that a company paid for my hotel room. Even though the event was right across the river from our office at the Sheraton in Arlington, I was excited about the new opportunity.

I tracked the attendance lists, processed payments, and created name badges. I was ready for my debut at my first event registration. To make the registration process more seamless, I thought it would be a brilliant idea to greet international attendees at the bar. It worked like a charm, and I handed people their badges and registration packets as I sipped a glass of wine. I met board members and chatted with them about the event.

Everything was running as planned, until I saw the chairperson give me a lingering look. I shook it off as a cultural difference, but I decided to shut down my impromptu check-in system anyway. Around 11 pm, I returned to my room with a full glass of wine. I was already tipsy, but I proceeded to finish my third glass on an empty stomach.

With bad reality television on in the background, I was drifting off to sleep. Then the phone rang.

"Hello?" I answered.

"Lauren…. Are you sleeping?" The suave voice inquired.

"Umm… I was about to."

"You better be, or I'll come up there and read you a bedtime story." He even rolled his R's seductively.

Chills ran up and down my entire body. It was wrong. So wrong. So very, very wrong. I reached for the remaining wine and took a swig. I needed to sleep, but my nerves were shot.

Nevertheless, I drifted off to sleep at some point. Then…

BOOM! BOOM! BOOM! "Who's in there with you?!?!"

I jolted upright and noticed a stream of light flooding in from the door. I charged at the door, but when I saw a large shadow filling the doorframe, I stopped in my tracks.

"Your door was open. Who's in there with you?" the bass voice asked.

"Umm... No one. I was asleep. Who are you? What's happening?"

"I'm with hotel security. Your door was open. Are you sure you're okay?"

"No, I'm not okay. I just got woken up because you were banging on my door. I'm freaked out."

"Sorry to disturb you. Go back to sleep."

But I didn't go back to sleep, and it was too late to call anyone. I was alone.

I crumpled into a ball on the corner of my king-sized bed, still wearing my clothes from that day. How did I go from elation and excitement to feeling like a violated victim? Nothing physically happened to me, but emotionally, I was shaken to my core, and I second-guessed all my previous actions. Was I too nice and friendly? Did I give someone the wrong idea?

My mind raced until my alarm went off at 6:30 am. With the speed of a car running on fumes, I took a shower and dressed for the day. I had a job to do, and I knew I needed to suck it up and put on a good face.

I went downstairs and sat at the registration desk, where I was alone again. None of my colleagues were on time. No one else stayed onsite. I felt exposed and raw. My nerves were rattled, but I tried to smile through each interaction. My glassy, bloodshot eyes told a different story.

Forty-five minutes later, support began arriving, since the CEO was making his appearance. He took one look at me and knew something was very wrong. It was my moment to tell the truth and expose the creepy chairperson, but I didn't. Instead, I told the traumatic story about the hotel door, which he quickly escalated to the General Manager.

Apologies swirled around me, and a plate of hot food arrived in front of me within minutes. I didn't tell anyone the other piece of the sleepless-night puzzle, but it soon reared its ugly head.

My 90-day review meeting was the next day, and I knew a raise was possible. Following a half-day meeting at the hotel, we all went back to the office, where my supervisor would give me the verdict. I eagerly sat across from her at her desk, which was piled with stacks of paper. She didn't look happy.

"Lauren, I have a word for you. Do you know what coquetry means?"

I sat there frozen as she reached into the folder in front of her and selected a ripped pull-off from the "Word of the Day" calendar she had on her desk. She read it verbatim:

co·quet·ry ˈkōkətrē, kōˈketrē/ **(noun)**

flirtatious behavior or a flirtatious manner.

"Watch yourself, little girl," she barked.

Was this seriously my review? Had everyone turned against me? What was happening?

She slid the piece of paper in my direction, to ensure I heard her message loud and clear.

Then it was if someone changed the channel. Her face brightened, and she happily told me I was doing a great job and would be getting a $5,000 raise.

"Thank you," I responded, trying to end this meeting as soon as possible. I left the room and the building. I was eager to keep moving forward and leave that unwelcome interaction behind.

Over the next three months, the pace of the job picked up. As we brought on three new clients, our six-person office grew to 15. And I sensed that a larger shift was about to occur. I'd only been there for six months, but I was ready to move up.

I learned how to manage budgets, run board meetings, take minutes, promote and market events, and work with multiple vendors and volunteers. I kept waiting for someone to tap me on the shoulder and give me a promotion, but it didn't happen.

When one of my three clients had an opening for an executive director role, my impatience grew. And when I discovered they were looking to hire someone from outside the company, impatience turned to rage, and I was ready to quit. "How dare they overlook me!" I huffed. I knew this role was meant for me, as I was already doing the work.

Thankfully, two allies emerged, steered me in the right direction, and encouraged me to apply for the position. Slowly, my ego quieted from a wildfire of entitled venom to a flame of determination. They both wrote me reference letters and reviewed my cover letter and resume.

When I found out the CEO was in town, I dialed up my confidence and asked him to have lunch. I filled an envelope with my future, and as we sat down in the restaurant, I placed it in front of him.

"So I know I've only done this job for six months, but I believe I can run this association. Here are letters of recommendation and my resume. You can remove me from the position at any time, if it turns out you don't think I'm up to it."

He looked shocked and intrigued. Apparently, my promotion strategy wasn't conventional. He opened the envelope and skimmed the documents.

"OK, it's yours. When we go upstairs, you can move into your new office."

It took all of my restraint not to jump up and hug him. Instead, I expressed my concerns about maintaining my previous workload.

"We'll figure it out," he promised.

We returned upstairs, and I started packing my items for my 15-foot move. As happy as I was about this change, apparently everyone didn't share my enthusiasm. During the process of moving, my supervisor (who'd accused me of coquetry) saw me and shrieked, "What do you think you're doing?"

 "I'm moving into my office."

She slammed her door in a fury, but there wasn't much soundproofing to quiet the huffing, puffing, and cursing. Then her door swung open, and she charged down the hall into the managing director's office with a stack of papers in hand. After twenty minutes behind closed doors, she definitely didn't get her way, and rampaged back down the hall toward her target: me.

"You little slut! You think you can stop working for me? Who do you think you are?!" Her voice increased in volume, and when she hit the top of her crescendo, she launched her stack of papers at me. At that point, two colleagues promptly ushered her back into her office.

Someone whisked me into another office, and I was notified when it was safe to reappear. She disappeared for the rest of the day, and soon left the company for medical reasons.

After that, my life was awesome on paper. I was a 22-year-old executive director with an office, and I had everything I asked for:

- More responsibility
- More money
- I was seen, acknowledged, and respected, and people stopped to listen to what I had to say.

I'd made all that happen. But even though my life was picture-perfect, I was anything but happy. It took me another decade to learn what true happiness was.

## Rediscovering My SpitFire Self

My picture-perfect life continued: Two years later, I met my now ex-husband, and I was in deep. He was a flawless specimen of health, fitness, and manners. And he was a good Texan boy with a rebellious side, and the tattoos to prove it. Within a year, we were living together and had an English bulldog named Rico Suave.

I'd checked off the box for my perfect-on-paper job, and now I was on my way to doing the same with my relationship. From the outside, it looked like nothing could go wrong. But then life happened.

When the Recession hit, it yanked the rug out from under me. And in January 2009, my employer went under. I had thirty days to find a new job, so I created a consulting company to manage my association clients. Still only 25, I shouldn't have taken on that amount of risk.

Thankfully, my clients saw the truth before I did. They understandably looked for other management options, but they also took care of me: I was set up at a 150-person association management firm, with the promise of growth, support, and mentorship.

But I wasn't out of the woods yet. Shortly after starting the new job, my live-in boyfriend called me and told me that he'd been let go from his job. We initially thought it would be a month or two of unemployment, but it turned into 13 months.

So for over a year, my paycheck covered all of our household expenses. I had a 90-minute commute from Fairfax, Virginia to DC every day, and I hated my new work environment. At my previous job, I consistently received freedom and praise, but they were replaced by skepticism and micromanagement. I was burned out, and the illusion of my perfect life was rapidly eroding around me.

I felt trapped by the expectation to take care of my family, but I didn't think I had any other options. I couldn't take the risk of being considered a job-hopper or ending up in a worse situation. The Recession had its grip on me.

Since I was afraid of losing everything, I retreated to the only option I knew: going on autopilot and tuning everything out. With every early-morning wakeup, mindless commute, and isolated workday, I felt my confidence and self-assuredness slipping away. I questioned who I was, and what I was meant to do.

But rather than focus on myself, I deflected my attention at where my relationship should be on paper. "Why aren't we engaged? We should be engaged!" I thought I needed a ring to make my sacrifice worth it or boost my energy.

I started subtly planting seeds by watching *Say Yes to the Dress* and *Four Weddings*. When that didn't work, I got belligerent and asked him when he was going to propose. It was time to check off that box.

Even though he was barely covering his bills with unemployment benefits, he cashed out part of his retirement to refurbish a ring that his second fiancé had returned to him. I justified the hand-me-down ring as "economical" and dubbed it a "green ring." But it felt like an afterthought.

This disappointment set the tone for our marriage. We'd started out as a happy couple who had a lot of fun together. But during the extended unemployment, a lot of sadness, stress, and depression crept in. I hoped that my feeling of obligation to take care of him and the little family we'd created would eventually be reciprocated, but that didn't turn out to be the case. We were both so concerned with surviving ourselves that a loving partnership was next to impossible, but it took some time before I could really see that.

Despite checking off another box, the picture-perfect Washington, DC life was no longer possible. After a while, we decided to move to Houston. I thought we could start a new life and put down roots there. It might be exactly what we both needed: a new place with new people. The way I imagined our new life, everything would be so wonderful.

But there was one problem: I hated Houston. First of all, the Magnolia City didn't result in more job security. Secondly, I'm from New Jersey. I need sarcasm and quick wits surrounding me. People in Houston considered my jokes to be insulting, which caused making friends to be quite the challenge. As much as I tried, being in Houston was like trying to fit a square peg in a round hole.

So we decided to try out another new city (Las Vegas) and another new business (CrossFit). What better place to strengthen a marriage, right?

Wrong! When we added a mortgage into the mix, things went from bad to worse. The house was enough to make anyone on Facebook jealous. It was my dream house: 5 bedrooms, 4.5 baths, and a casita (which is like a guest house that's attached to your house). With every like and envious comment on Facebook about what we'd accomplished, I glowed with pride. "You're the perfect couple." "You're so successful." "You have it all."

But the compliments were a temporary way to fill a deepening void. I surveyed my happiness checklist to see what was missing:

- ✓ Work-from-Home Career

- ✓ International Travel

- ✓ New Business

- ✓ Massive House

- ✓ Picture-Perfect Relationship

- ✓ Cute Dog (Seriously, look at this dog!)

*(This is my dog, Rico Suave. He's a lot bigger and older now, but still as adorable.)*

What was missing?

My Purpose. My Passion. My Fun. My Creativity. ME!

Every day, I felt the weight of my responsibility increase. If I didn't think I could leave my job three years before arriving in Las Vegas, there was no way I could do it with a new house and a new business. To make matters worse, my ex-husband was horrible at time management, and could barely make it to the gym to open on time.

I knew we had to take care of members to keep the business open, or we'd lose the house. So I got certified as a CrossFit Level 1 Coach, and started spending my days at the gym. I would wake up at 5:00 am, and either coach at 6:00 am or start my East Coast work hours online. If it was the latter, I'd pop into the gym to make sure the mats and bathrooms were clean, and the customers were taken care of. Either way, we'd share coaching duties for the evening classes, so my days didn't end until 9:30 pm.

Now factor in my expectation of what a coach was supposed to look like. I was expected to workout 4-6 days a week and "eat clean." I hated working out and internally felt a competitive nature to be the best, so people wouldn't notice I was faking it. I felt like a fraud, but I didn't see any other options.

I worked 16-hour days for a year and a half. Then I hit my final wall.

My mom is the best BS sniffer I know. (Thankfully, I've inherited that wonderful trait.) When she visited me for a long weekend, we went out to eat at a local Tex-Mex restaurant. I usually order a salad, but that day, it was queso-laden nachos.

"Are you emotionally eating?" she joked.

I snapped. "I just want to fucking eat these. Am I allowed to do that?"

She gave me a look and didn't need to say anything. My outburst confirmed that I wasn't okay or happy, but she also knew there was nothing she could do until I acknowledged I needed help.

The next day, I dropped her off at the airport and drove to Phoenix to run an annual convention for one of my association clients. I was completely frazzled. I'd never felt so off my game. My onsite team was amazing; they had everything prepared when I arrived.

Instead of resting, I used the opportunity to binge-drink at the pool (and everywhere else I could). I wanted to forget my life. I wanted to be free, but I didn't know how.

I'd never gotten this drunk at a work event. I'd been tipsy, but never blackout drunk. On the final day, I drank by the pool for two hours, then stumbled down to our St. Paddy's Day networking reception. I could barely stand up or walk straight. Before I knew it, I felt tears coming and couldn't stop them.

I knew I was going to be sick, so I retreated to the farthest bathroom to avoid the attendees. I was gone for about thirty minutes, which was definitely long enough for my team to notice. At some point, I must have blacked out, because the hotel staff picked me up in a golf cart and drove me back to my hotel room.

My dress was soaked in tears, booze, and bile. I called my husband, but he didn't answer, which he rarely did. Even if he had answered, I wouldn't have heard what I so desperately needed: affection and validation.

Somehow, I sobered up enough to change my dress, wash my face, and make my second attempt at the reception.

I apologized profusely to my team, and I knew I needed to make big changes. The next day, the meeting planner and I drove to Palm Springs for a site visit, and we talked everything out.

After a hard look in the mirror and deep reflection, I decided to work with my dad's career coach, who I thought would help me find a new job and get my happiness and sanity back. My new coach was the first real investment I'd ever made in myself that wasn't on my checklist for being picture-perfect.

During the first hour-long session, he asked me a series of open-ended questions. I got frustrated because I wanted him to give me direct guidance. "TELL ME WHAT I'M SUPPOSED TO DO!" I screamed internally.

For 31 years, I hadn't thought about what made me happy or passionate, beyond checking off boxes for school, job, and relationship. I didn't know there was a box for purpose/passion, which I could create on my own. During my first session, the option of making my own choices and defining my own journey awoke. Now I had options, and there was no turning back!

After one month of weekly coaching sessions, I realized that my limiting beliefs and marriage were making it impossible for me to be happy. My coach didn't give me the answers, but asked questions to find out where my thoughts, beliefs, and actions were coming from. I'd been operating under so much stress for so long that I could only see one way to live. Then after a month of concentrated focus, I could see options emerging.

We worked together to create a personal mission statement, which flew out of me within the first few minutes of the meeting: **I AM A CATALYST FOR POSITIVE CHANGE.** (I created a canvas painting of my mission statement, and I keep it on my bathroom wall to remind me of what I'm here to do every day.)

My coach and I played around with what I wanted to do for work. I described my dream of consulting and supporting brands (individual and corporate). I wanted to light a fire under people to be their best selves, and have the creative freedom to be innovative and playful with the people I work with.

"You're meant to be a coach, Lauren," my coach said, with decades of wisdom behind him.

"Nah. I'm not a woo-woo Life Coach." I sneered.

"Go do some research about it. Then you can judge it."

That's exactly what I did. Over the next few days, I did deep online searches about what it took to be a coach. I scheduled a phone interview with an admissions counselor at iPEC (The Institute for Professional Excellence in Coaching). I quickly realized that their practical and applicable approach to coaching was more my speed than sitting in a classroom and regurgitating information.

When the price tag came, I gulped. I didn't question that it was a good investment, but I knew I had to share the news with my husband. I took a deep breath and walked downstairs to the kitchen, where he was making a protein shake.

"So after working with my career coach, I've decided I'm going to be a life coach!" I proudly proclaimed, naively assuming everyone would be excited about my decision. "It's a lot of money, but I can put it on my credit card, then pay it off before I'm done with school in 8 months."

He stopped stirring and looked up at me. I thought he would be pumped to hear about the personal growth I'd made. A dark cloud had been looming over him for months, and I thought this awakening would be a breath of fresh air for our relationship.

This train of thought was extremely inaccurate. To the say the least, he wasn't supportive. In fact, he thought it was a joke and started chuckling to himself. "It's your money. Do what you want, but don't think you're going to quit your job and coach people at the gym."

It was like a kick to the gut. All the positive energy that had lifted me so high popped in an instant. Suddenly, I could feel how different we truly were. His response had nothing to do with me. Rather, it had everything to do with his fear of his wife changing and impacting his financial security. To regain my focus and clarity, I retreated up to my office and journaled for a while.

I didn't need his approval (or anyone else's) to do what I needed to do. I knew who I was. I was following my passion and purpose. It was the first time I filled out my own permission slip, and did what I wanted AND needed to be happy.

As our conversation about becoming a coach continued over the next four weeks, more truths were exposed. He admitted he didn't want to have children, and didn't see anything changing in our situation. In fact, he didn't want anything to change. His exact words were: "Why isn't this good enough for you?" He wanted to stand still forever, but my journey was just beginning.

It really was like my purpose had been asleep my whole life, but was now awake. And it didn't involve 16-hour days, thankless work, and an empty relationship with no hope for progress. I felt like I was suffocating and had to get out. I needed a new partner who wanted to walk along my new path with me, and I knew in my heart that we would never have that kind of partnership. By the end of that month, the divorce documents were filed and approved.

I don't think you ever really get over divorce. You work through the emotions as you transition to a new normal, but the scars and pain of past breakups can creep in during your most vulnerable moments. It becomes part of your woven fabric.

I had to ask myself: Are you going to choose to learn lessons and create a new path, or recreate the same cycle?

I chose to dig deep and use my awakening to break everything open and expose what I'd been hiding for three decades.

I got divorced at the end of April, and I hit the ground running. I was a woman on a mission. Working with my coach, I built and executed a transition plan. Each week, I felt a dial-up of my inner fire.

I enrolled in coaching certification with iPEC and started classes in mid-July. That first day changed my life. Within three hours, we were tapping into our inner critics and biggest fears (also known as Gremlins).

We each wrote down a word that symbolized our greatest fear on a thin piece of Styrofoam. My word was ALONE. I stared at it. Then I heard the messages streaming through my head. "You'll always be alone." "No one wants you." "You're unlovable." "No one sees you." "No one cares." I cringed and cowered, afraid of what was coming next.

The facilitator announced that we would share our word with everyone in the room. My body convulsed, trying to hold back the emotion, but it was too much to tame. There in a meeting room with thirty strangers, I lost my shit and started crying uncontrollably. I was essentially airing out my dirty laundry, and I felt exposed again.

But instead of sexually harassing me, throwing a stack of papers at me, or calling me a slut, this group surrounded me and shared their fears with me. They had their own words on their own Styrofoam to deal with. It wasn't about me anymore. It wasn't about my secret. We were all dealing with pain from our past. Some were better at covering it up than others, but everyone understood that they weren't the only wounded people there.

At that moment, I realized that I wasn't alone. I was INDEPENDENT, POWERFUL, and BRAVE. I thought I knew I wanted to be a coach before, but the power in that room locked it in.

On the third day, we performed a meditation. I sat on the floor against a wall, and realized I'd never really meditated before. Maybe it was the emotional exhaustion, the openness, and the trust, but I was fully into it. During the guided meditation, I felt a bright white light wash over me, and then it hit me: **YOU ARE THE SPITFIRE COACH.**

The voice began as a whisper, then progressively built in volume until it was a guttural scream: **YES! I AM THE SPITFIRE COACH.**

The week after the coaching weekend, my tagline emerged: **UNCOVER YOUR TRUTH AND YOUR FIRE, ONE CONVERSATION AT A TIME.**

So, ladies and gentlemen, that's exactly what we're here to do: Uncover your truth and your fire, one conversation (or chapter) at a time. And I'll help you express it!

# Chapter 2

## Redefining SpitFire

Before we get into the inner workings of The SpitFire, let's spend some time on the definition. Shortly after I launched The SpitFire Podcast for Creative Entrepreneurs and Passionate Professionals, I started writing this book. Before guests came on the show, I asked them to answer the following three questions:

1) Do you consider yourself a SpitFire?
2) What's your story?
3) Should we avoid any topics?

All but one said they thought they were SpitFires. (I'll get to the outlier in the Frequently Asked Questions section.) At some point in the interviews, I asked them to define what they thought a SpitFire was. They used adjectives like bold, courageous, resilient, passionate, confident, strong, creative, and fearless. No one took offense to the term. In fact, many used it as a badge of honor.

But if you type "spitfire" into Google, you'll get the following definition:

| **Spitfire (noun):** |
| --- |
| a person with a fierce temper |

That doesn't sound like a very friendly person, and I don't think that's what my great uncle had in mind when he called me one as an impressionable six-year old.

I decided to keep looking until I found a suitable definition. The one on Dictionary.com wasn't much better:

**Spitfire (noun):**

a person, especially a girl or woman, who is of fiery temper

and easily provoked to outbursts.

Hmmm…. Now I'm starting to feel offended. What's with the gender attachment, Dictionary.com?

You don't need a history lesson to know that strong women haven't always been treated with wide acceptance. Often, derogatory terms were created to label wily, ambitious loudmouths who made others uncomfortable. This sentiment still lingers unfortunately.

How many words or phrases exist that are used to stifle power? The word "spitfire" had no negative connotation when I heard it as a child, but the dictionary and history books were filled with gender-based blocks and walls. If you're a bold and outspoken woman, you have fiery outbursts. So you mean to tell me that every time I'm confident and speak up for myself, I'm going to burn down the village? Or every time I disagree with someone, I'm going to make them cry? I didn't realize I had so much untapped town-destroying power!

I decided to give it one more go and turn to my Old Faithful online resource, UrbanDictionary.com:

---

**Spitfire (noun):**

1.  Someone that's wild & free, and can say what he/she wants to say without a care in the world

2.  Someone whose angry words sting like fire

3.  In some cases, can be considered a Cimarron

4.  Also, considered strong emotionally & spiritually

5.  Someone who you don't want to be on the bad side of

6.  Someone whose angry words are like fiery ice

7.  Fiery

---

Now we're getting closer, but it still needs a little work.

Since the online dictionaries want to put a negative spin on it, I decided to create my own definition with a more positive and accurate spin. Here is how I define a SpitFire:

> **SpitFire (noun)**
>
> 1. Someone who is emotionally and spiritually strong, and can say and do whatever he/she wants.
>
> 2. Someone who is full of power and passion, and exudes and inspires confidence.

This last definition is applied to numerous products: the Supermarine Spitfire (fighter aircraft), the Triumph Spitfire (sports car), Spitfire Wheels, Spitfire Skateboards, Spitfire Clothing, and (of course) The SpitFire Podcast.

This word evokes a response. It's powerful and projects a feeling of unapologetic action and delivery. It's not a passive or dainty word. It's meant to make you feel uncomfortable. If you're feeling uneasy right now, sit with it. I promise that you'll emerge stronger by the end of this process.

Here's what it comes down to: You can define a SpitFire however you want. You can be inspired and motivated by it, or you can be offended and take it as an insult. I choose to find the power in the words I use, so let's get in touch with the force of your fire.

**Why Do I Capitalize the "F" in SpitFire?**

1) Because it's my book.

2) Because it looks cool.

3) Because it's the same word in spelling, but in this version, it stands for more passion, more power and more awesomeness and none of that nasty gender negativity.

# Chapter 3

# Elements of The SpitFire

Words have power, but so much more goes into being a SpitFire than a definition. In this chapter, we'll examine the elements of The SpitFire. To keep it simple, we can break down the term into two parts: Spit and Fire. Let's start with the second part of the phrase: Fire. Then we'll cover the first: Spit.

## Fire

What is Fire? According to Oxford Dictionary, fire is a process in which substances combine chemically with oxygen from the air and typically give out bright light, heat, and smoke. But, don't worry there will be no flint or gasoline involved in this book or fire breathing for that matter.

When I started looking into the hidden meanings of being a SpitFire, I researched how fire was made and maintained. I was inspired by the logical nature of balance and integration that create a sustainable reaction. I recreated this fun image, which represents the four aspects of making fire:

# The Fire Tetrahedron

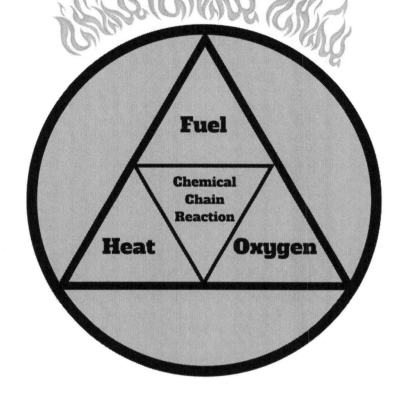

The Fire Tetrahedron is made up of Heat, Fuel, Oxygen, and a Chemical Chain Reaction. If you're interested in learning more, here's a video from my old school favorite, Mr. Wizard!
(https://www.youtube.com/watch?v=kGGUNM9D78A)

I used this real-world reference to create The SpitFire Tetrahedron, which we'll use for the rest of the book.

# The SpitFire Tetrahedron

Similar to The Fire Tetrahedron, The SpitFire Tetrahedron needs three key elements to create a fourth reaction. While the former relies on fuel, heat, and oxygen to create a chemical combustion cycle, The SpitFire Tetrahedron relies on passion, motivation, and Self-Care to create your power.

Here's a chart to simplify the translation of terms:

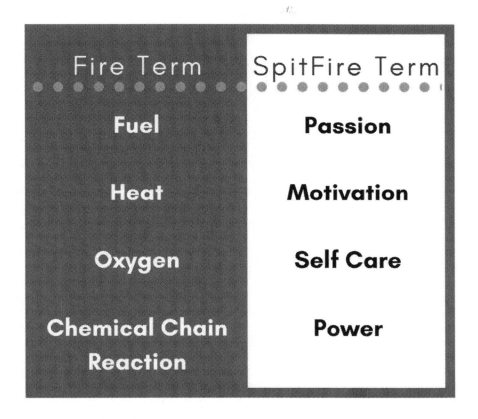

| Fire Term | SpitFire Term |
| --- | --- |
| Fuel | Passion |
| Heat | Motivation |
| Oxygen | Self Care |
| Chemical Chain Reaction | Power |

Now that we have pretty pictures and translation grids, we're ready to dig deeper into what these elements mean for you.

## Fuel = Passion

By definition fuel is any combustible material: solid, liquid, or gas. Passion by definition is an intense desire or enthusiasm for something. Internally, your passion is shaped by your history, belief system, skill set, knowledge, culture, and family. It includes all the elements that make you who you are, and that can trigger you. Because this is one of your core elements, it has the highest probability of being a sensitive button that can create a reaction.

One of my clients has been an artist her whole life. She majored in art in college and has spent thousands of hours (probably years) in front of a canvas. Soon after college, she put her brushes away and couldn't create the art she once did. When we first started working together, she couldn't pinpoint why she was so unhappy. She was in a great relationship, had a full-time job, and was thinking of starting a family. When she thought about creating art, she was sad that she wasn't using her talent and passion, but she was too burnt out to try.

After working through her blocks around past family grief, financial security and judgement, she was able to pick a brush up again. She told me it felt like electricity was running through her veins. As of this book, she has just launched her creative business making snarky art with a cause-driven angle.

Although dormant for years, her passion was always there. By working through these blocks, she was able to ignite her love of painting and get back to what mattered.

Yes, this take on the journey is very simplistic, and it's still ongoing. The key takeaway is that your passion doesn't go away, even if you don't use it.

If you don't know what your passion is, don't worry, we'll have exercise to help you explore this area later on in the book.

## Oxygen = Self-Care

Similar to fires, we need oxygen to exist. Fires only need an atmosphere of 16% oxygen, but humans need at least a 19.5% concentration. Fires need oxygen to breathe and exist; without it, the fire is snuffed out. Guess what? The same thing happens to us! If we don't breathe and take care of ourselves, we lose our power, motivation and ultimately BURN OUT!

### Self-Care Can Be as Simple as Focusing on Your Breath

The first time I did karaoke, I picked my favorite hip-hop song: "Rapper's Delight" by Sugar Hill Gang. If you've ever heard the song, you know that it's 6-12 minutes long, and it's performed by three guys, for good reason. In my bold and naive thinking, I decided to take on this behemoth. The first verse was a piece of cake:

"I said a hip hop

Hippie to the hippie

The hip, hip a hop, and you don't stop..."

You get the idea, right?

I kept going for another four verses. At that point, two emcees are supposed to take over the load of the song, because most people would be gasping for air. My voice got shallow, and my throat felt like it was closing up. I knew the words by heart, so it wasn't anxiety or nerves; it was my breath control. I kept pushing and tried to squeeze out another line. Then I hit a wall. I couldn't sing any more. My voice was shot, and I was super-dizzy.

In this example, my lack of breath lead to my premature karaoke demise. Without oxygen, you can't perform or make people boogie. Shoot, you can't even stay upright. But think about how much you hold your breath throughout your day, trying to make everything work. It's exhausting.

I've been referring to breath a lot because it's a major component of Self-Care. It's an indicator to your emotions and deeper beliefs about the situation. Shallow, short breath can be a sign of stress, exhaustion, anxiety, anger, or frustration. Even-paced breath can show comfort and security. Slow, deep breath can be a sign of deep relaxation, peace, and creativity. You'll know best what your breath means to you, but it's really important to start paying attention to it now.

## Self-Care Practice

Self-Care can be as simple as meeting your basic needs, such as ample sleep and a healthy diet. Your enhanced Self-Care practice can be added into your existing schedule, including meditation, exercise, journaling, reading, dancing, and telling jokes. Notice that I mentioned practice. So many of my clients get tripped up on the consistency of the practice. We're really good at focusing on days, weeks, and months, but maintaining a lifestyle that supports and celebrates Self-Care can sometimes be a challenge.

When we don't get enough sleep or take time for reflection, movement, and enjoyment, our ability to be focused and motivated becomes a chore. Just like your breath, when you can focus on the frequency and feedback from your Self-Care practice, you can self-assess and correct your schedule, activities and influences. Instead of becoming frustrated because you can't figure out when you have no motivation or energy, you can analyze your Self-Care to see if it's the reason for the drop-off. If you're on track with your Self-Care, you can look at your Passion, and see if you need more work in your values or take a look at the next element in The SpitFire Tetrahedron: Motivation.

# Heat = Motivation

According to Dictionary.com, heat is a form of energy arising from the random motion of molecules, which may be transferred by conduction, convection, or radiation. To start a fire, enough energy has to be present to increase the temperature of the fuel to the point that it gives off sufficient vapors. Then ignition can occur. Without a sufficient amount of heat, the integrity of the fire can be compromised.

So how does heat fit into The SpitFire Tetrahedron?

In our SpitFire model, "Heat" is relabeled as "Motivation." You've heard this old theater-actor reference: "What's my motivation?" That simple question directs us to the energy that we take in and exude.

**Catabolic vs Anabolic Energy**

Whether we're sitting in reflection or sprinting to the finish line, everything we do is rooted in some level of motivation. This variable becomes the energy that we either react to or fight against. That's right, we have the ability to shift our motivation and our output of energy, which is where the coaching principles of iPEC come in.

In iPEC's Core Energy Coaching, we focus on two types of energy: catabolic and anabolic.

Catabolic is most prevalent in stress reactions (fight or flight). It's great for short-term results, but on a long-term basis, it's exhausting and unsustainable.

Think about the last time you got into a heated argument. Your blood was boiling. You raised your voice. You were focused on winning and getting your point across. After a few minutes, you were probably exhausted— emotionally and physically. You may have been temporarily charged up, but for the next few hours or days, you felt like crap. These effects are most likely due to catabolic energy.

Unlike catabolic energy, anabolic energy is focused on growth and enhancement. (Think of steroids making your muscles bigger.) The more anabolic energy you give off, the more it's drawn back to you and the better you'll feel on a long-term basis.

Have you ever made someone laugh? How is it different from laughing alone? When everyone is laughing together, it feels like a high. Think about the last comedy show or funny movie you saw. When others are sharing in the same joy, it's an exponentially more enjoyable experience, which makes you buzz for hours.

Anabolic energy isn't as quick or powerful in reaction compared to catabolic energy, but it is more sustainable in the long term. Runners who are conditioned for sprints need short bursts of energy in small amounts of time. It's imperative that they get moving quickly, with a big burst of energy. In 20 seconds, they've expended a huge amount of energy and need time to recover.  On the other hand, marathon runners have trained to keep a sustained pace over a long period of time. They find their minute-per-mile sweet spot and go into an almost meditative state. They cover a lot of ground, and some even get a runner's high along the way. At this pace, they run for hours, and their breath is controlled. After sprinters cross the finish line, they're gasping, because they've exerted their maximum effort.

## Enough with the Sports Analogies. How Does this Relate to Me?

When you know where your energy is coming from, you're more equipped to control and sustain it if you choose to. Are you passionate about something, but find your motivation fizzling out over time? If so, here are some key questions to explore:

- What makes you feel inspired?
- When you are starting a new activity, what are you inspire by? Could you be reacting to something?
- When you do something, what role does approval and validation play?

If you mentioned approval, validation or feedback as your motivation, you may want to explore your values and passion on our upcoming exercises.

If your passion and breath are in alignment, your energy may need a mindset shift or a cohesive strategy to execute your dream.

## Chemical Chain Reaction = Power

As defined by our pyro-loving friends, the Chemical Chain Reaction is a self-sustaining series of reactions. Power by definition is the capacity or ability to direct or influence the behavior of others or the course of events.

When we combine our first three elements and we can watch the magic happen. When we tap into our passion, breathe, and engage in anabolic energy, we can create a cyclical reaction that sustains itself.

When all elements are intentionally activated, you'll feel the powerful flow of being a SpitFire.

## The SpitFire Equation

Here is our SpitFire Tetrahedon Equation:

> **Passion x Self-Care x Motivation = Power**

Each component is reliant on one another for its intensity, effectiveness, and sustainability. That's why it's important to be aware of your energy sources, environmental impacts, and areas of external influence. We'll review this content in the following sections. So hang tight!

If this section seems airy-fairy, I totally get it. When I was going through coaching training, I thought everyone was taking bong hits between sessions. But I couldn't fully tap into my inner fire until I started shifting my blocks around judgment and my limiting beliefs around success.

Now that we've covered the Fire, let's get to the Spitting part!

## The Art of The Spit

Here's the simplest, least gross definition I was able to find:

> **Spit** (verb): to eject from the mouth

But, I'll offer an even more pleasant definition:

> **Spit** (verb): to express with passion

If you aren't a dope MC like JRSY FRSH, you don't need to spit fire onstage. You can express your fire through a number of activities like writing, dancing, painting, math, sculpture, cooking, or staring contests. The way you express yourself becomes the vehicle for your fire.

For me, the way I spit my fire is by speaking, performing, and asking catalyst-provoking questions. Once I knew I wanted to be a coach, I couldn't ignore it or suppress my inner fire and I had to express it. When your fire finds an opening, it flares up until it can come to the surface and be noticed.

At first, I thought this effect was specific to my experience, but the more clients I worked with, the more I saw SpitFires at work.

### The Improvising SpitFire

I worked with a stay-at-home mom who was feeling dejected about not being able to find a job. She'd been away from the corporate world for three years, and she'd lost her confidence and vocational passion.

I challenged her to try something new. "How is this going to help me find a job?" she questioned. "Our goal is to shift your mindset, in order to prepare you to show up as your best self in the job search," I replied.

She begrudgingly took on the challenge. About a month later, I heard from her. "OMG! I did improv storytelling for the first time, and I won a competition." She was excited, but also had a new level of self-awareness about how she thought about herself and her situation. By finding her voice and being able to express it, she was able to shift her perspective from the passenger seat to the driver's seat.

For my client, it was improv and public speaking. For you, it could be something you've never tried. So seize the opportunity to make a list of activities that scare and intrigue you.

# Chapter 4

# Current State of Your Fire

Your fire is yours, and only you know its current state. Notice I didn't mention the size of your fire. Size doesn't matter. I repeat: SIZE DOES NOT MATTER.

What does matter is your intention behind the intensity, quality, and source of your fire which is related to your Motivation and Self-Care. You have the ability with your intention to increase or decrease the intensity of your power. You can think of your intention as your "Why".

Let me break it down for you like this: Imagine you have a dial. It's not an on-and-off switch, but it does allow you to turn your flame to full brightness or darkness.

When your dial is turned all the way up, you can see everything around you and feel the warmth of the light. But if you stay in the light too long, you may end up over-exposing yourself or burning the bulb or your senses out. If this were an actual fire you would burn and a larger and hotter rate.

When your dial is turned all the way down, you can't see much around you, and you don't quite know what to do. You'll use less energy, but the benefits of warmth and visual clarity are much less.

I sense that trying to figure out which setting you need to strive for is causing your brain to go into overdrive. Let me stop you right there.

**SPOILER ALERT: THERE IS NO "RIGHT" SETTING.**

**I repeat: THERE IS NO RIGHT SETTING.**

This pill is usually hard to swallow for our insta-fix mindsets. But before you throw this book at the wall in a fit of rage, here's some more information to sink your teeth into.

Each setting on your dial has benefits and challenges. To simplify further, I've broken down your inner fire into three phases: Ember, Flame, and Blaze.

## Ember

*Passion: Low*

*Motivation: Low*

*Self-Care: Low*

*Power: Low impact, but longest duration potential*

The Ember requires the lowest level of fuel, heat, and oxygen. As a result, it has the lowest level of impact, but the potential for the longest duration. It's the most common type of fire I encounter in everyday life.

While the Ember is low-risk, low-energy, and low-impact, it can create a lot of frustration and anxiety especially once your awareness to your potential appears.

## My Ember Cover-Up Story

Take my story as an example. I knew I was meant for a life with more impact than the one I was currently living, but I couldn't pinpoint my passion and purpose, which led to frustration and resentment.

I lived in a hidden state of Ember for 15-20 years. On the surface, I was smiley, outgoing, and fearless. But at home, I was afraid of being discovered as a happiness imposter. I didn't feel clever enough, and I spent most of my time developing schemes to fool people into thinking I was more experienced than I was.

I exhausted myself, trying to read people's minds or decode what they could be questioning about me. My external fire may have seemed powerful to outsiders, but my internal fire was barely ablaze. The embers in my heart had almost been snuffed out, since I wasn't living my life in alignment with my internal values.

Everything I did was focused on preserving my forced identity. If I did anything for myself, my true motivation involved making someone else happy. I didn't work out for mental clarity; I did it to be more physically appealing to my partner and members of the gym. I didn't read for intellectual curiosity; I did it to be able to regurgitate facts and seem superior to my colleagues and peers.

During my 20s, if you asked my family, friends, or coworkers to describe me, they would probably have used words like "determined," "competitive," "driven," or "successful." In fact, I modeled my behavior and vocabulary to focus on these achievement-based values.

If I was busy doing tasks, no one would ask me how I was really feeling. My happiness was contingent on the wins or accolades I received, not on any deeper purpose or intention. I was a high-functioning Ember.

And social media sure isn't helping the Embers out there. Every post reminds you that you should be happier. And look how easy it is in three easy steps! No one else has the same financial worries, family obligations, and unappreciative boss that you have. This comparison mentality only piles more guilt and judgment onto the buried Ember.

You may be reflecting on your own situation and trying to assess whether you're in a state of Ember. Here are some questions for further exploration:

1) When was the last time you felt happy?
2) On a scale of 1-10 (1 being low, and 10 being high), how happy were you?
3) On that same scale, how happy do you feel right now?
4) Typically, how long do you feel happy?
5) Is your happiness contingent on someone or something? If so, who or what is it?
6) When you feel the most passion, what brought it out? You, a situation, or another person?

These questions will give you some clues about what may be blocking your passion, and how to resolve it. Take some time with these questions. (They changed my life.)

## Flame

*Passion: Medium*

*Motivation: Medium*

*Self-Care: Medium*

*Power: Medium*

Imagine a candle burning. Look at the flame. If given enough wick and space to drip wax, the flame is consistent. But if it's in a windy room, the flame flickers, so it's at risk of being blown out. If it's in a container that doesn't allow for wax to drip away, the flame can drown it out. If given too much wick, the flame can grow to a dangerous level.

There are tons of factors at play in maintaining your Flame, but to keep it simple, we'll focus on three key areas:

1) **Your Passion**
   Why does it motivate you? How does it motivate you?

2) **Your Source of Energy**
   Are you motivated by reacting and proving people wrong? Are you 100% motivated by your greater cause?

### 3) Your Breath and Self-Care

Your Flame can only be maintained if you're taking care of yourself. Your breath is the key to the health of your Flame. If you're huffing and puffing while chasing your passion, it's less likely that you'll be able to maintain it. But if your breath is full and deep, your Flame will have more than enough energy to maintain it.

You may be thinking that the Flame is an awesome place to be. It burns constantly, and doesn't require as much structure to contain it. It's also very safe, predictable, and small. It's known and understood, and there is little to no risk associated with it. But the backlash is that it doesn't create growth, change, or impact. It makes moves, but is more focused on maintaining the norm. The only phase that drives big change and impact is the Blaze.

## Blaze

*Passion: High*

*Motivation: High*

*Self-Care: High*

*Power: High*

For this high-impact, high-energy, high-passion, and high-maintenance fire, the dial is turned all the way up. If you've ever been around a roaring fire, you know you can feel the heat from far away. To avoid getting burned, you may keep your distance. As you look at the base of the fire, you notice that it requires constant fuel and nurturing to maintain its intensity.

The Blaze has the highest impact for change of all the levels. With this intensity, it can spark other fires and provide heat for many people, and it can be seen from far away. The Blaze wants to be noticed and felt.

The Blaze also has the greatest chance of creating destruction. If you've ever seen a fire left unattended, the risks can be catastrophic and destructive. It scares people, and when it feels out of control, people try to put it out. In this explanation, I'm talking about actual fires, but let's apply it to your inner fire.

*Think about the last time you were extremely passionate about something.*

Let's say you want to plan the ultimate vacation for your family. You work hard every day, and you don't feel appreciated. So you need this vacation to be epic. You do tons of research, set the budget, purchase the tickets, and type up the itinerary.

All your energy seems to be forced into one train of thought. Nothing can get in your way. With a super-focused vision of what you want, anything less than what you imagined is a failure, and it's unacceptable. If someone denies you or disagrees with you, he or she may receive some colorful language.

In the end, you're successful in your endeavor, but as you look around, there may not be many people nearby. Your epic vacation is a perfect reflection of your plan. But you and your family are exhausted, and you're barely speaking to one another.

When catabolic energy is influencing your Blaze, every element of your fire is at a ten. You should feel energized and happy, but you don't. This impact is a tell-tale sign of catabolic energy.

Do you have the notion that every action, thought, and belief must be right and perfect? Is there only one way to do things? If so, you're only left with two options: succeed or fail. That mentality sets you up for a stress reaction. While you may feel energized at the front end, you're anything but rested by the time you've accomplished your goal.

*Let's consider another example.*

You have two deep passions: building communities and painting. You've had an internal itch to use art to connect kids with their communities. This nagging feeling keeps popping up and growing in momentum.

Soon, you notice others around you who have skillsets that could launch your project, or connections in your community that could provide space and supplies. The more you show up and talk about your idea, the more people and resources emerge to support it. Each day, your focus and motivation grow, and your idea eventually becomes a reality. Your ability to trust others and ask for support has transformed the seed for an idea into a self-sustaining program. Sure, you have moments of doubt and concern, but you know you're making a real difference and have a team supporting you and the vision.

This Blaze is sourced by anabolic energy. The motivation is grounded in a sustainable source: your passion. The more open you become to opportunities and support, the more it's attracted to you. At times, you feel like things are flowing to the point that you're only along for the ride. Even when you have dips in energy, you quickly rebound to focus on your goals and vision while remaining in the driver's seat.

What difference do you see between these two examples?

What examples in your life are emblematic of each one?

We all have flare-ups of energetic expression. They could be rage, passionate exchanges, or flailing limbs. Trust me, I won't judge you. I know I get fired up, and I react to stress on a regular basis. I also know when I'm truly rooted in my passion by being creative and inspiring others to be their best selves. When this situation happens, I attract opportunities and people who inspire and motivate me, just like a magnet. With energy, like attracts like. When you know what you're putting out, you can have more control and awareness about what you're attracting.

I encourage you to spend some time reviewing the Fire types below, and examining where your energy is coming from. Later, other exercises will help you explore your passion and values a little deeper.

# Ember

| Pros | Cons |
| --- | --- |
| • May be unaware of potential<br>• Ignorance can be bliss.<br>• Low (or no) expectations<br>• Low-maintenance | • Untapped potential<br>• Low (or no) energy<br>• Lack of motivation and drive<br>• Uninspired<br>• Low (or no) impact |

# Flame

| Pros | Cons |
| --- | --- |
| • Sustainable heat<br>• Consistent and dependable<br>• Motivated and driven<br>• Sustainable impact | • Requires more fuel<br>• Requires maintenance<br>• Requires structure<br>• Higher Expectations |

# Blaze

| Pros | Cons |
|---|---|
| • High-impact | • Requires high levels of fuel |
| • High passion | • Requires ongoing maintenance |
| • High motivation | • Attracts attention from fire-snuffers |

**What level does your inner fire feel like it's on today?**

**What level do you want it to be on?**

**What ideas/strategies do you think would adjust your level/**

# Chapter 5

# Discovering Your Inner SpitFire

If the other sections seemed a bit abstract, this section is going to start connecting the dots for you. When I walk clients through these exercises, the lightbulb moments are plentiful. You may feel frustrated or overwhelmed right now, and that's totally normal. When you're having a stress reaction (such as frustration, anger, or resentment), it immediately blocks your ability to be creative. Let it be and focus on deep breathing.

**Stress and Creativity**

Think of a time when you were overloaded with a pile of projects and ticking timelines. Perhaps it was at your current job or when you were in school. One of those projects required you to design a new concept for a company. Your email was blowing up, your phone was buzzing away, and people kept popping into your office to ask you for more work.

How much energy and creativity did you have to put towards that concept? Probably none. Even the thought of it probably creates stress, which is overwhelming.

Now imagine that you have a quiet, organized space with two hours to solely focus on the concept. Your email and phone are on "Do Not Disturb," and no one will bother you when you have your door closed.

In this situation, how much focus and energy do you have? I'll bet you have a hell of a lot more.

It's interesting: We expect to perform at the same levels when we're stressed out as when we feel calm and organized. Under stress, we react to the most immediate need. Without stress, we can objectively look at the situation and examine our options. But under stress, we feel like we only have one option.

Are you feeling like you can't find your passion, or you don't know what it is? If so, don't worry; it will come to you when you're ready. If you're stressed out or burned out, you may need to breathe and take care of yourself, not put another project on your plate.

Before you explore your dreams and passions, let's start with your foundational values. Your values are the elements that drive everything you think and do. You can think of them as your compass or true north. When you understand your values, you can prioritize and set goals that mean more than a trophy or ribbon, and you feel fed on a deeper level.

Your values may be influenced by your family, friends, religion, or environment. When you look deeper, you may realize that you don't want the lessons you've been taught. Remember that itch we talked about earlier? That's your true value screaming to come out.

## Values Exercises

In the following exercises you'll have a chance to explore words that inspire, drive and influence your actions and decisions. We'll start by selecting those words and then we'll peel back some layers to see how those values may or may not be working for you in comparison to your goals and intentions.

## Step One: Values Compass

Do you know what your values are? If you don't or you can't think of any, don't worry. I've compiled a list of options for you review right here: www.spitfirecoach.com/s/Values-Worksheet.pdf

1) Review the words or come up with your own and select the ones that speak the most to you. (Aim for 10 words) They're the words that motivate, inspire, and drive you to make or avoid a decision. Write them down here.

_____        _____

_____        _____

_____        _____

_____        _____

_____        _____

_____        _____

2) Take a look at your values. You may notice that some words are similar. Feel free to consolidate them down to six words here:

_____        _____

_____        _____

_____        _____

3) Now that your list in narrowed to six words, write two sentences about how each word motivates and impacts you in your daily life.

| Value | Impact/Motivation Description |
|-------|------------------------------|
|       |                              |
|       |                              |
|       |                              |
|       |                              |
|       |                              |
|       |                              |

4) Now let's take a look at where you think each value came from. A family member? Religion? Your peer groups? Society?

Value: _____ Origin: _____

Value: _____ Origin: _____

Value: _____ Origin: _____

Value: _____ Origin: _____

Value: _____ Origin: _____

Based on your descriptions, you may be able to streamline your list further. If you're feeling solid about your words, think about which words drives you the most. This is your most core value.

Core Value: _____

How does your core value connect to your other values?

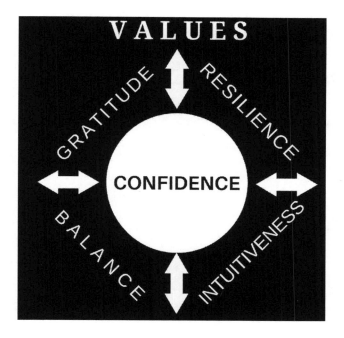

Here is an example of a Values Compass I created for one of my clients.

After her value assessment, we found that her core value is Confidence, which is fed by Gratitude, Resilience, Intuitiveness, and Balance. Each value flows into the other, but her value system is fueled by Confidence.

Feel free to plug in your own values and create your own shape so you can pinpoint your core value and see how all the values interact to make you who you are.

Congrats on completing Step One! Now let's examine how those Values are and aren't working for you.

## Step 2: Value Engagement

In this section, we're going to examine the language you selected when you were describing your values. Keep your value descriptions nearby. We're going to use them for the next few steps:

1)  Using your descriptions, circle or highlight any of the following words and phrases that appear: "Can't," "Won't," "Need To," "Have To," "Want To," and "Choose To."

2)  To determine how those values are adding to or detracting from your energy, take a look at the following grid:

| "Can't" | "Have To" | "Need To" | "Want To" |
|---|---|---|---|
| No Power | Forced Effort | Low-Power | High-Power |
| No Choice | Limited Choice | Mostly at Choice | All Choice |

**"Can't "**

On the left side of the grid, we use words like "Can't" in our description. When we use this term, we feel and express no power and no choice. Life is happening to us, so we may feel out of control or powerless about making decisions or looking for other opportunities.

**"Have To"**

Next to "Can't" is "Have To." While we have a little more power, our effort is forced, and takes a lot of energy out of us. We feel like we have a limited choice of options, if any at all. Usually, we act in fear of a potential consequence, or we muscle our way through to get it done. There's no joy or fun here, just hard grunt work as we're explaining it to other people. Even if it's unintentional in its usage, "Have To" can have residual impacts on motivation our over time.

"Have To" is usually rooted in expectations or learned labels from our family, friends, and society. We say we "have to" do something, but do we really know why? We assume the role and actions associated with "Have To," but when we use the phrase in our language, a clear conflict in our personal values emerges.

**"Need To"**

It's more powerful to "need to" do something than to "have to," as there is more of a connection to the purpose behind the action. It's usually connected to a greater goal or larger vision. When we frequently say we "need to," we're aware of our choices, and we look for opportunities when challenges arise. However, frequent distractions can deviate us from our desired course.

For example, you cringe at the thought of managing your finances in your business. Every time you think about reconciling your expenses and following up on invoices, you feel overwhelmed and stressed out. You remind yourself that you "need to" manage your books and collect invoices, but don't feel motivated to get it done. Instead, you rip the band-aid off and force yourself to do it.

In this example, you know why these tasks are important, but the frame you use to describe the action feels like a chore. (When working with clients in a "Need To" mindset, I call these items "Eating Your Vegetables.")

When locked in a "Need To" mindset, a solution for increasing your motivation and engagement is to ask yourself what you really want to do, and what you're willing to do to enjoy your situation more. Using our example of finance management, what do you enjoy about invoicing and doing the books? What do you detest about it? What could you delegate to someone else? What could you do to enjoy the process more?

When we become aware of what we want and why, we can shift our power into a more effective state.

**"Want To"**

This level of language engagement is the most powerful. At this level, people are fully engaged, because they feel they have the full power of choice. They enjoy their roles, and they're absorbed in them. And they feel a powerful connection between who they are and what they do.

What do I mean by "role"?

Throughout our lives, we are assigned roles, such as sister, father, cousin, student, comedian, and entertainer. While these labels are usually harmless, we take on the expectations that are associated with them.

As we grow and learn about our passion and purpose, we can redefine our roles. We can be an artist, educator, connector, or adventurer. The roles we want to have are the ones we feel most powerful in.

For example, one of my clients is a mother, wife, designer, and problem-fixer, and she frequently felt burnt out and overwhelmed because she was trying to solve everyone else's issues. After exploring the areas and roles she felt most powerful in, she recognized that she loved being an educator. Now when new issues pop up, she goes into an educator role, so she can better navigate her stress while maintaining her power level—all because she chose that role.

**Growth vs Fear-Based Values**

Our language choices provide clues to the feelings behind our values. We can see the shift in power with the range from "Can't" to "Want To." We can go even deeper when we look at whether our values are based on growth or fear. Because our responses originate from past experiences, our values influence what we avoid or attract in future situations.

**Fear-Based Values**

Let's say my primary value is "security." It allows me to feel safe and confident. It keeps me away from people who try to **hurt** or **take advantage** of me. I **need** financial security. I **need** to know that my bills are paid, and that I'm protected. If I don't have security, I feel **vulnerable** and **at risk**.

In my description, I've highlighted "hurt", "take advantage" "need", "vulnerable," and "at risk". That's a lot of fear embedded into my description. My driving word is "need," which motivates me to get moving. Even though I know that I spend a lot of energy avoiding a negative experience, the fear-based value inspires me to act.

**Do you see any fear-based values on your list?**

In your values descriptions, I would encourage you to go back and think about how often this value has shown up. Did you feel empowered? Was something outside of you pushing you to think or act?

If you're using words like "not" or "never," go back and rewrite your description in a positive format.

Perhaps you said, "I never want to feel like I'll be taken advantage of." If so, you can rewrite it to say, "I choose the people in my life who respect and value me."

So how do you determine what your values are based on?

Here's a simple way to determine the difference between fear-based and growth-based values:

Fear is focused on the past; it tries to prevent situations from repeating themselves. Growth is focused on feelings and intentions in the future. Fear-based values are littered with catabolic energy, and growth-based values are overflowing with anabolic energy.

Which of your values are fear-based?

_____          _____

_____          _____

_____          _____

And which ones are growth-based?

_____          _____

_____          _____

_____          _____

You can rewrite any values and descriptions to reflect the energy you want to attract. Before moving on to the next exercise, spend some time rewriting them now. Feel free to use a separate piece of paper.

**Pro Tip:** You definitely shouldn't tattoo these words on your back (unless you really want to). Your values may change and evolve over time, based on your experience, reflection, and understanding of yourself.

# Passion Exercises

The following sections provide you with more insight and tools to tap into your passion, including The Wakeup, Reflection, and Future Visioning.

## The Wakeup

A lot of my clients have described the discovery of their passion as "waking up." They're going about their daily lives, and something happens that opens up a new way of thinking. Once they see what's behind the curtain, they can't un-know or un-see what they saw. A consciousness awakens: You've always been aware of it, but you couldn't see it.

When we "wake up," our awareness dial is turned to a level that allows us to view what's prevented us from seeing our surroundings. In other words, we may notice a mirror that allows us to see ourselves in a new way, so we may be able to reflect on what has transpired.

### What Triggers Us to Wake Up?

I had a debate with my friend about triggers and wakeups. Her theory was that we have to hit rock bottom, in order to see everything above us. I disagreed. While some people have made huge shifts after rock-bottom experiences, I think a crack or a tiny opening in a person's armor allows a question, an experience, or a person to provide a clue that things may not be what they seem.

My wakeup happened after my career coach asked a question during our first session. "When do you get to be happy?" This one question changed the course of my life. I'd been faking happiness for so long, I didn't know what made me happy anymore. I also didn't feel like I could be happy in my current situation. As soon as I acknowledged that I was the creator of my happiness. I started to see other areas in my life I could control and change.

A wakeup shows you the truth, but the work only begins there. I notice that a lot of people get extremely confused and frustrated after an epiphany. At first, everything seemed so clear and easy, but they try to apply concepts and tactics from the past to make everything work (i.e. playing a new game with an old set of rules).

With anything new, it takes time to adjust. Change can be scary, and the unknown can make you anxious. Throughout this process, I encourage you to be curious and talk to a professional to help you work through it.

## Reflection

After you read these instructions, I want you to close your eyes. Take four deep breaths. For six seconds, inhale deeply through your nose into the lower part of your belly. Then hold it for another six seconds, and slowly exhale it from your mouth for six seconds. If you can only do four seconds, start with that. And if you can do longer, go for it.

After your breathing exercise, notice what your body is feeling. Do you feel pressure in your shoulders, forehead, neck, or lower back? Keep breathing. If you're feeling relaxed, you can move on to the next portion.

Keeping your eyes closed, think back to the time when you were happiest. You felt light and filled with joy. In this moment:

- What were you doing?
- Where were you?
- Who was around you?
- How old were you?

Now pick three words that describe how you felt during that time.

1) _____

2) _____

3) _____

Why are these words important to you?

1) _____

2) _____

3) _____

On a scale of 1-10 (1 being low, and 10 being high), rate how each of these words show up for you in your life now.

1) _____ Score: _____

2) _____ Score: _____

3) _____ Score: _____

If you have a 10, what do you do to maintain that feeling?

_____

_____

For the words that you rated with less than a 10, what activities or projects could you realistically do to increase that number?

_____

_____

This simple exercise can be used for any activity at work or home. When we focus in on what truly makes us happy, and why it makes us happy, we're practicing the highest level of Self-Care.

You may be scratching your head, or feeling even more confused. So let's try another exercise.

## Visioning

Close your eyes again. Imagine that it's 10 years from now, and you're super-successful. You're at a dinner table with your closest friends and family, reflecting on your journey over the past decade.

Now ask yourself these questions:

- What are you saying?
- Why are you successful?
- Who's there?
- What do you feel?
- What have you accomplished?
- Why did it make you feel successful?
- Which of your values are being served? How?

# Motivation

Energy exists everywhere around us. Without it, we wouldn't be here. Here's the way the OxfordDictionaries.com defines energy:

---

**Energy (noun)**

the strength and vitality required for sustained physical or mental activity

---

If you're into physics, you know that energy either expands or collapses on itself. Even when energy is stored, it either grows or dies. We're made up of cells and atoms, which create energy in their simplest form. In basic elements, energy is positively or negatively charged. We're no different.

The energy we create through our thoughts, beliefs, actions, and reactions have a positive or a negative impact on our lives. If you think you can hide from this principle, good luck! Even if you hide under your covers, you're still making a choice and taking an action. Your energy is directly correlated with your motivation.

Why is this correlation important to your inner SpitFire? Your energy is the source of sustainability, intensity, and vitality. If your energy is reactive, it's fed by external factors. If your energy is proactive and purpose-centered, you are the source.

*For this example, lets imagine you have a passion for connecting kids with their communities.*

Let's say you've tapped into this passion and started volunteering a local community based non-profit part-time. You have a full-time job and a growing family at home. At first you were excited to take on every project you could get your hands on, but now you find yourself feeling exhausted at the end of the day, and wondering if anyone cares.

Your buddy Charlie at the non-profit sends you email after email about all the issues in the community that need to be fixed, and these solutions are clearly in your wheelhouse. Your mind starts racing about what will happen if you don't address those issues. Will your initiative fall apart? Will the community collapse?

You frantically respond to each email with a commitment to focus your efforts on singlehandedly solving the problems. Before you know it, your passion project that was supposed to take 5-10-hours has turned into a stress-filled nightmare. You're dropping the ball at work, missing deadlines and taking your stress home. No one is happy.

What's going on here?

Your intentions were spot-on, and you checked your passion box off. But the source of your motivation may have been externally driven. You may have relied on the smiles of kids or the high fives from city council members to fuel you up. You may have relied on Charlie to tell you if you were doing the "right thing." These options pulled you away from your internal motivation, which was rooted in your purpose.

When you experience an influx of distractions and conflicting opinions, how do you stay rooted in your purpose?

Your values and mission statement are your purpose. They're your reason why. They're you.  No one is going to know the inner workings of you— not even your mom. You are unique, and that's awesome. You don't need validation from anyone else to be you, or to work on your passion.

**Let's be clear: Feedback is NOT Validation.**

Feedback should be requested and received—without judgment or expectation. This mechanism should collect alternative perspectives and give you a comprehensive strategy. Feedback should increase your creativity and options, not limit or diminish them.

However, validation involves chasing acceptance. "Am I ok?" "Is this ok?" "Do you like me?" "Am I good enough?"

If you feel yourself needing validation, start by asking, "Why am I questioning myself?" Then dig deeper for the answers to the following questions:

What do you know, without a doubt, about yourself?

What makes you a rock star?

When you can tap into your strengths and call in your SpitFire evidence, you don't need that external validation. It's the sprinkles on your awesome sundae.

## Your Permission Slip

If you take anything away from this book, know that you are more than enough, and you always have been. You have always had a permission slip in your back pocket. You don't need anyone's validation, because you are awesome.

Now think about your passion. What have you been afraid of, or needed permission to do?

Congratulations, you're now free to follow your passion! Do you *need* to parachute out of a plane? No. But if you really want to, go for it. That side project you've been meaning to start is right there. That book you've been wanting to write is waiting for you!

You don't need me to tell you, but I will.

You see, my SpitFire superpower is reigniting the SpitFire in you. I give you permission to go and do the things that will make you even more awesome. My purpose is to be a catalyst for positive change. My energy is based on infectious and positive growth.

I've been called crazy, and a lot worse. Some people aren't inspired by my perspective, and that's okay. That's the beauty of being human: We're all different, so we can enjoy different aspects of one another. I know at my core that I'm in the flow pocket of my purpose. And when my inner SpitFire is dialed up and cared for, I am unstoppable.

**What do you do if your energy is rooted in reaction?**

Go back to the Values Exercise, and spend some time on your descriptions and the words your selected. If they don't fit for you, pick new ones. If your descriptions include words like "Can't," "Won't," "Need To," "Have To," "Want To," and "Choose To," change your phrasing to "I Am" or "I Want To." You have the ability to create power in the words you choose. This exercise is no different.

Own your internal statement. Repeat it daily or hourly, or even every minute. What do you need to do to remind yourself of who you are, and what you were meant to be? Whatever it is, DO IT!

By not being you and working within your passion or purpose, you're preventing others from experiencing their joy. When you hold back, others hold back. But when you tap into your passion and joy, you can also infect others with positivity and courage.

# Self-Care

I've listed Self-Care last to make sure you remember it. In my opinion, Self-Care is the most important, overlooked, and underappreciated element in The SpitFire Tetrahedron.

When your priorities shift, your Self-Care practice is the first to be ignored. Think about the last time you were slammed at work. What changes occurred in your Self-Care habits? How were you sleeping? How often were you exercising? What did your diet look like?

I bet you saw a lot of things fall off your list that you "just didn't have time for."

You were probably exhausted, but just couldn't make the time to decompress before sleep, which led to tossing, turning, and getting less than 6 hours of sleep. So you tried to compensate with copious amounts of caffeine and energy drinks, which made you feel icky. And you didn't have time to plan out your meals, so you picked up fast food on the way home and felt even ickier.

What do you think you needed most at that moment? How could a ten-minute break change your outlook? What if you could've gone for a walk?

"I'm too busy. That's wasting time." Is it?

Go ahead and try it. When you're feeling busy, go for a walk without your phone. Start with five minutes (or ten, if you want to live on the edge). Just walk around, and focus on deep breaths.

If you're like me, you're going to have tons of ideas on that walk, but things you "have to do" will rush in. Let them come and go. At the end of the walk, the ideas that stick are the ones you can choose to act on.

These ideas are due to our good friend showing up: catabolic energy. It keeps us reactive and short of breath. All of those "urgent tasks" distract us from our bigger picture. I'm not telling you to be inactive. I'm telling you to breathe and be objective.

## List Overload

Are you creating an insane list of "Have Tos"? Why?

What does being able to say "You're Busy" give you? A distraction? An excuse?

What if you could choose your next move? Guess what, you can!

But first, you need to stop the noise, and turn off the distractions. You need to make your purpose a priority. You need to give your inner SpitFire the space and oxygen it needs to grow and flourish.

Let's try a short exercise.

# Mind-Body Task List

I'm sure you've heard about the Mind-Body Connection. This exercise will help you connect the dots between your task list and your body's reaction:

What's on your task list? When you think about each task, where do you feel it in your body? Is your chest tight? Is your forehead throbbing? Do you feel a weight in your shoulders?

This reaction is totally normal. This energy is based in catabolic stress. You've created a pressure cooker of presumed impossibilities, and your brain is overwhelmed by them, which creates anxiety.

Can you guess what worry is? It's an obsession with future outcomes.

Can you guess what you control about your future? Not a damn thing, except your actions in the present.

Instead, we waste our time, running scenarios:

- "How is Jane going to react to this presentation?"

- "What is Bob going to do when he sees the latest sales report?"

We cannot control or predict others' reactions, yet we distract ourselves with events in the future that we can't control.

(Deep breath. In through the nose for a six count. Hold it. Hold it. Out through the nose for a six count. And repeat.)

Hopefully, your heart rate has returned to normal.

See how your breath just reduced your stress? MAGIC!!!!!

Let's use that breath to objectively direct our action plan:

1) Write down your task list for today on a separate piece of paper or in Excel.
2) Highlight the "Urgent Fires That Have to Be Put Out Today."
3) Create two lists. One for "Urgent Fires for Today" and one for "Semi and Non-Urgent Fires"
4) Next to each item, write down how long you think it will take to put out each fire.
5) Start with the most urgent and work your way down.

You should only focus on today. And if you awesomely achieve those items on your urgent list, you can move onto your semi-urgent tasks.

**Pro Tip:** If the task seems too overwhelming, you need to break down the goal into smaller tasks and actions. If it takes longer than 30-minutes, break it down into small time block tasks.

If this focus doesn't work, you can try this tactic: the value-connection qualifier. You can repeat the above steps, then go one step further, and refer back to the values list you created. Next to each item, write down the value that was served by each task.

It's amazing: Even the most trivial tasks can connect back to your values:

---

**Task: Go to the Bank to Deposit Checks**

Priority: URGENT

Time Needed: 15 minutes

Value(s): Play, Passion

Results: By depositing these checks, I'll have more cash flow to play with. Then I can tap into my passion without worrying about money.

---

Now you can try it while focusing on your breath.

Your breath is at the core of your Self-Care. It's the first symptom that your Self-Care is at risk. A shortness or tightness of breath is a cry for attention. First, it will whisper. Then it will talk. Then it will yell. Finally, it will scream until you're paralyzed and silenced. Your body knows what it needs, so listen to it the first time, will ya?!

When you're firing on all cylinders and taking care of yourself, you become more powerful and can better navigate the challenges that come your way.

You'll have tons of "Chumbawamba Moments." If you're my age or older, you'll remember their hit song from the 90s, "Tumbthumping." The chorus was: "I get knocked down, but I get up again. You're never gonna keep me down." If you have no idea what I'm talking about, google it!

The true sign of a legit SpitFire is elasticity. When you're rocking the Self-Care, you can bounce back, learn grown and inspire other SpitFires!

# Chapter 6

## Connecting to Your Fire

In the previous section, we dove into your values and tapped into your passion. So now what? That passion has always been there, but now it feels like it's in a glass case. You stare at it with curiosity and confusion. You scratch your head and pace around it, and frustration mounts as you increase your lap count.

You want to scream. Go ahead and do it!

Release that frustration. Release those expectations. Release that pressure. Your life isn't a race or a competition.

When you feel overwhelmed and frustrated, here are some simple steps that will connect you back to your inner fire:

1. **Take a deep breath, and do nothing.**

   Don't think about what you should do.

2. **Go have fun.**

   Find your joy. Whether it's playing in the mud, painting your fingernails, or doing the running man, go be silly. When you can release those endorphins, your creativity will expand.

3. **Schedule quiet time.**

   If you don't currently meditate, try it for a minute or two. If sitting still isn't for you, go for a walk, and focus on a color. With external silence, we can hear internal messages.

Your brain will start to freak out, and it will try to tell you everything you should be doing. Resist the urge to get distracted. Sit in the silence.

4. **Listen to what your inner critic is really saying.**

What do you need to do to take care of yourself? What have you been putting off or ignoring? Your health? Your sleep? Your water intake?

When you're taking care of yourself, your inner critic is nowhere to be found. When you hear someone saying you "should" do something, do nothing except listen.

After you've addressed him or her, think about what life would look like if you tapped into your passion.

Recently, I had a Life Strategy Session with a client. He'd just moved to California to start a new job. As a goal-focused, self-professed "Type A" professional, he felt the need to have a specific plan in place for his next phase. We went through the same exercises that are in this book. He had a strong passion for efficiency, problem-solving, and startups.

After breathing through the need to accomplish everything that day, we played with options about how his passion could grow in his current work and life. As soon as he felt permission to not be perfect, we arrived at his solution.

By putting his experiences, passion, and values on paper, he could connect the dots and create a comprehensive idea that fulfilled his creative, professional, and growth-based needs. His idea may change over time, but soon, he'll be firing on all cylinders without burning out.

Here's another Key Principle for you:

**When your fire is based on your values and passions, your sustainability and power increase.**

# Chapter 7

# Spitting Your Fire

Now that we've discovered and connected you to your inner fire, what do you do with it?

You may be feeling some residual frustration from the last chapter. We're trying to move years and decades of acquired stories and limiting beliefs, so give yourself a break. You've done some serious heavy lifting.

You aren't in a rush. Patience is your friend. You may feel antsy, and want to go change the world.

Are you feeling tightness in your chest, and hearing words like "should" and "must"? If so, remember that your first step is to do absolutely nothing. In the long run, the urges to do and be without a grounded foundation of passion and purpose will result in inefficiency and lost momentum.

Remember when we talked about catabolic energy as a source of motivation? It's that reactive and sometimes defensive energy that protects us from perceived threats. This type of energy is very common during your Spitting phase—if you aren't paying attention. That's why your first step is to do nothing. Sit in the space of not knowing, and be okay with it.

After I got certified, it took me over a year to feel confident, comfortable, and secure about expressing myself as an expert. I worried that people questioned my validity and experience, and in turn, I questioned if I could make it as a full-time coach. I wanted someone to give me a manual on how to believe what I didn't know, but I really needed to trust myself and listen to my inner fire.

After I sat in silence for 5-10 minutes, I would let my brain dump everything out on paper. Anything that popped into my head, I wrote it down. At first, it looked like a task list. Then the self-doubt and fear came through.

I got really emotional during those solo sessions, but then someone amazing happened. I looked at the words on the page, and I began seeing opportunity in my fear. Instead of burying it, I embraced it and addressed it. I put my fear in the forefront, and started writing about it, which gave me more confidence to start a blog, host a podcast, speak to rooms full of people, and write this book.

Your fire can be expressed any way you'd like. You can make music, paint, sing, dance, problem-solve, build communities, create nonprofits, take care of animals, debate, research, teach, speak, or write. There are no limits.

If you're unclear about how to express your fire, go try something new, and listen to your body when you're in that moment. Where do you feel it? What does your inner critic tell you? On a scale of 0% to 100%, how powerful do you feel?

Let's say you love to write, but you feel stuck about what to do next. Set a timer for 10 minutes, and write down all of the ways you could use your writing to express your passion. There are no wrong answers or expectations. After the timer buzzes, go through your list, and circle three ideas that you immediately gravitate towards.

Give yourself a reasonable timeline, and try one, two, or three ideas out over that time. If it feels awesome, stick with it. If the method doesn't work for you, note what did and didn't work about it, and move on to another option if you choose to.

You can read tons of books and blogs and watch YouTube trainings, but they're all other people's experiences that build their playbooks. Today you have the opportunity to write your own rules.

If you don't express your fire, you can become frustrated and stifled. If outward expression isn't for you, look for outlets that allow you to express ways that support your values. Maybe it's a small group of like-minded Mario Brothers enthusiasts. Maybe it's a group of crocheting octogenarians. Find the environment that supports your expression.

**What groups/activities are you really interested in?**

**What steps are you willing to take in a week, month and/or year to pursue your interests?**

# Chapter 8

## Maintaining Your Flame

I hope your passion has been reignited, and you're inspired by the new ways to Spit Your Fire! This section of the book highlights potential challenges to your fire. It includes ways that you can maintain your passion and power, even when fire-snuffers enter your environment.

Before we get into the tools and tactics to maintain your fire, I want you to understand that this exercise doesn't involve finger-pointing or blame-games. I'm a firm believer that all elements have positive and negative sides; they balance us. As a coach, I'm not 100% perfect and positive all the time. I judge people and things. I get rejected and don't want to get out of bed, but I eventually do, so I can tap into my SpitFire powers.

The same is true for people who challenge your fire. Usually, the people closest to you only know one version of you. Perhaps they know you as that cute, bratty, little bookworm who keeps to herself and reads in a corner. Then one day, you tap into your power, and suddenly, they don't recognize you because:

- You cut your hair.
- You're wearing new clothes.
- You're hanging out with different people.
- You're speaking in new terms.
- Your body posture is totally different.

"Clearly, this change isn't going to last," they think. Or they may even say to you, "It's just another fad."

What does it say about them if they don't believe in you and support you? Is your relationship still valid and valuable?

Here's what can end up happening:

People in your life may challenge your new, positive outlook to see if it has staying power. If you maintain your power and root into your purpose, these people will either get onboard or filter out. It happens all the time, and it can be hurtful. But it's okay. Would you rather be happy with three fewer friends, or miserable and surrounded by people who don't really know you?

I've experienced this situation in my own life, and I see it happen with my clients as they own their power. I wish it didn't have to be painful, but I promise you that you'll be fine!

## Identifying Your Motivation Boosters and Suckers

In the SpitFire Tetrahedron, Motivation is one of the four necessary elements for creating and maintaining your fire. Like an open door or uninsulated window, energy can leak out at different intensities. Imagine that you have a fire burning in the fireplace, and you leave your front door wide open. How warm would your house be?

Now think about your life in the same context. Where do you feel most cozy and supported? Where do you feel most energized? Maybe it's a fitness class, a park bench, your home office, or your church. I call these locations your Environmental Energy Boosters.

Write your Environmental Energy Boosters here:

_____

_____

Now think about your Environmental Energy Suckers. Which places make you feel heavy and anxious? It could be your workplace, a family member's house, or a place that evokes a negative memory.

Write your Environmental Energy Suckers here:

_____

_____

In addition to your environment, the people around you can boost your energy or suck it from you. People are rarely neutral in this way. When you think of the people you encounter most, who increases your energy, supports you, and inspires you? And who drains your energy?

It's not an all-or-nothing situation, but there are both positive and negative impacts. You can think of it as a scale. You enter a situation, and approach people who are giving off positive or negative energy. Depending on the weight of their energy and your ability to hold your own, the swing of impact can skyrocket you into joy and creativity, or plummet you into frustration and despair.

Like all these areas, being aware of positive and negative influences will allow you to create a strategy and cope with them.

This situation may sound very abstract and idealistic. If I meet an icky person, I just avoid them. But what happens when the people who suck the most energy from you are your coworkers, parents, or friends?

## Motivation Boost/Suck Assessment

Here's a helpful exercise to see how people in your life impact your energy. On a separate piece of paper, write down the people you encounter on an everyday basis, including the cashier at the grocery store and the security guard in your building. List everyone on that piece of paper. Then use a plus (+, ++, or +++) or minus (-, - -, or - - -) system next to their name.

If you feel super-awesome after you see them, write down +++. If you feel like doo-doo on the side of the road, write down - - -. Here's an example:

1) Nick (Significant Other): + + +
2) Fluffy (Dog): + + +
3) George (Security Guard): +
4) Newspaper Lady at Metro: + +
5) Cindy (Boss): - -
6) Jane (Coworker): - - -
7) Paul (Coworker): ++
8) Francisco (Cafe Owner): +
9) Becky (Friend): +++

From this list, you can see the parts of your day that have the potential to boost or drain your motivation.

It looks like the first part of your social day is awesome. Then once you get to work, you feel depleted, but you have an ally (Paul), an escape strategy (the cafe on the corner), and a boost talking to your friend (Becky).

This exercise is intended for observation, and I strongly recommend destroying it once you're done. If the people on the negative side get a hold of it, it's not going to end well.

What are your options when dealing with negative influences? Here are the steps you can use to handle these influences:

1. **Acknowledgment**

   Acknowledge that both positive and negative energy exist. Perfection does not exist, and you will be faced with obstacles and challenges throughout your life. If you're expecting rainbows and unicorns floating around, I hate to break it to you, but that's not realistic (unless you're in a chemically induced fog). Remember, people are doing the best they can with what they have.

   Also, acknowledge that you're not all good or bad. But something within you is unresolved, which leaves you open to being triggered.

2. **Assess**

   What's your intention in the situation? How can you show up to get the best outcome? Do you need to nod your head and shut your trap? Do you need to speak up and defend yourself? Do you need to acknowledge and validate others? Do you need to listen?

   Can you objectively look at the situation, and evaluate your role in it and your impact on it? If so, you can create a game plan to maintain your energy.

3. **Exit Strategy**

   Know when it's your time to go. Listen to your body and take care of it. If your blood starts boiling, get out of the situation and go for a walk. If your chest starts tightening, excuse yourself, go to the bathroom, and catch your breath. If someone is a known Energy Sucker, manage your exposure and the frequency of your interactions.

4. **Reflect**

   After you've left a negative situation and caught your breath, reflect on everything you felt. What was said and/or done? What triggered your negative reaction? What are your options moving forward? Can you steer the conversation toward a more positive topic? Can you disengage from the intensity? Can you get out of the other person's story? Can you practice better Self-Care before the interaction?

What's in your power? You only have control over your mindset, beliefs, thoughts, and actions. You have the power to choose who and how you engage, but you don't have power over other people and their actions.

## The Power of Saying "No"

Why is this word so hard to say? Why does it make us feel like we're the scum of the earth if we use it?

It's hard for me to say it sometimes, too. I want to make people happy. I want them to like me, but let's keep it real: If I say yes to you when I want to say no, I'm really saying no to my priorities and happiness.

So where does this resistance to saying no come from? And what can we do about it?

As kids, we were experts at saying no, much to our parents' frustration. Do you want more applesauce? "NO!" Do you want to take a nap? "NO!" Do you want to take a bath? "NOOOOOOOOOOOOOO!"

Back in the day, we were "No" Stars. Then something happened: peer groups.

We started to care about how we fit in, and what people thought about us. We started listening to that inner critic that told us we weren't being good enough, smart enough, funny enough, or nice enough. And we went deep into the rabbit hole of being liked, instead of respected.

When Jessica asked you to go to the mall, you wanted to say no. But then the FOMO (fear of missing out) bells started ringing. Never mind that you had loads of homework to knock out and hadn't slept in three days. To feel like you belonged, you had to keep up appearances.

As young as second grade, I felt like I had to show up and say yes to be liked. As I got older and started Happy Hats, it only got worse. I said yes to any opportunity that came my way. Need a hat in 20 minutes? You got it! Need 50 hats in a week? Not a problem.

I never stopped to think about the impact that all these yeses were having on my physical, emotional, and mental health. I was always exhausted, and I was sick every other week. I never felt like I could catch my breath. It was a race to a finish line that never appeared.

Now you could call this situation a "grind" or a "hustle." And from the outside, it looks like hard work, but internally, it was a traction-less quest to be accepted and liked. It was 100% externally driven.

By the time the option of saying no entered my life, I was hitting rock bottom. But fortunately, I'd just started working with a coach. After working 16-hour days for almost two years, I realized that I'd "yessed" myself into an unhappy corner.

Without being properly compensated, I was taking on more responsibilities at work, hoping they'd someday appreciate me with their bank accounts (instead of their empty words). I was coaching CrossFit and struggling to look, feel, and act the part, hoping that the members would buy into my "healthy" example.

I was searching for people to tell me everything was ok, so I could possibly believe it one day.

Clearly, "fake it till you make it" wasn't an effective strategy for me, and coming from a place of "yes" was overloading my plate.

When I was able to pause and ask myself what I really wanted, there was a whole lot of "no" in my life. Before I could feel confident exercising my "no," I had to get to my why (my values, passion, and purpose). I also had to get to the limiting-belief blocks that were driving me to say "yes" to things that weren't working for me.

This work was uncomfortable and painful, but the more I tried, the easier it got. I used creative strategies that ranged from a subtle "I think I'll pass" to a hard "hell no!"

When my job asked me to take on another client, I wrote up a proposal, which included three reasons to give me a raise. After they offered me half of what I requested, I thanked them. Then I resigned six weeks later.

When my husband informed me that he no longer wanted to have children, I contemplated what that life would be like. Then I told him he didn't get to make that decision for me, and we were divorced within three weeks.

When my friends asked me to go on an expensive vacation after I'd just started my company, I let them know that it wasn't in my budget. But I clarified that they should tell me when they were doing something more local.

When I knew what I wanted, I could clearly communicate what I didn't want without engaging in emotional or reactive behavior. If it didn't feel right, I didn't do it, but I also gave the offering party an explanation and an alternative.

It's amazing what happens when you can say no without expectations about the outcome, or fears about what someone will think about you. It's not always 100% effective, but over time, you start shifting your values from others to yourself.

Think about the last time you said yes when you wanted to say no.

What feelings of guilt or fear came up?

What does it say about you if you say no?

What's driving you to say yes?

If you could say no, what would it allow you to say yes to?

Give yourself the time to get back to someone. Say you need to check your schedule. Say you have to check with your spouse or significant other. Say your mom might be in town. Say whatever you need to say to create distance, so you'll think before you react.

## Connecting to Other SpitFires

Over time, as you uncover and unveil your inner SpitFire, other SpitFires will naturally gravitate towards you. You may have met these people before, or they may be complete strangers. As you become more confident and powerful, others with confidence and power will naturally be attracted to you. When new people come into your space, keep the prior section in mind around energy impacts. Initially, these people may seem like SpitFires, but under the surface they may have energy sucking tendencies. Trust your gut!

I'm not telling you this to make you skeptical or paranoid, but I do want you to be aware of your motivation and power. As you create your own SpitFire Network of Awesomeness, think about the boundaries you want to set for your time, energy and resources. Create an intention and a list of the qualities you want to attract.

How do you know when someone else is a SpitFire?

What do those individuals bring to the table? What do you bring to the group?

What are the deal-breakers?

Once you have a SpitFire or two in your circle, others will follow, and it's up to you to decide how much energy you invest in maintaining that circle. Remember your breath and Self-Care. When others are fully in their anabolic, SpitFire energy, they don't require maintenance or micromanagement. They have their own flow. They'll call you when they want to play, and you'll say yes when it works for you. But SpitFires in catabolic energy will seem high-maintenance, needy, and intense.

Why am I making this point? I want you to acknowledge your energy source, and what you're projecting. Then you can attract amazing energy that will enhance your awesome impact on this planet.

### The SpitFire Circle

Once you're finished reading this book, I'd love to have you join The SpitFire Circle: a virtual and DC-based community of powerful SpitFires that focuses on sharing, supporting and expressing one another's passion projects. Feel free to check out the following link for more information and to sign up for a future group: www.spitfirecircle.com

## Setting Boundaries

Once you've identified the Energy Suckers, it's super-duper necessary to set boundaries, which are great ways to create limits on the energy you put out and take in. Think of boundaries as your first line of defense for energy-invading forces.

One boundary for you might involve getting home from work by 7 pm, so you can get a good night's sleep and prepare for the next day. You may have coworkers that want to extend happy hour, and keep the good times rolling. But you know if you say yes to one more drink, you'll be there until 8 or 9 pm, and your quality Self-Care time will be replaced with a hangover in the morning. Now factor in that important board meeting that you wanted to prepare for and nail down. It'll now be a source of anxiety and stress.

To create clear boundaries, go back to your Values Exercise. What's important to you, and why?

List your values in the chart on the next page. Next to each value, write down what you need to do to honor that value. What values have you been overlooking in your current routine and interactions?

| Value | Activities |
|---|---|
|  |  |
|  |  |
|  |  |
|  |  |

Here's an example:

| Value | Activities |
|---|---|
| Connection | Monday Night Potluck, Volunteer, SpitFire Circle, Daily outreach to friends and colleagues |
| Community | Monday Night Potluck, Volunteer, SpitFire Circle |
| Play/Adventure | Paint, Write, Walk the dog, Be silly, Dance, Spend time with friends |
| Peace | Yoga, Journaling, Meditation |

But what about family interactions that leave you emotionally exhausted? Uncle Frank keeps picking political fights, and Cousin Sue is always going on and on about her dysfunctional love life. How do you set boundaries in your family?

Think about your values again. How do you honor them? When interacting with people who don't honor your values, how do you honor them anyway? Let those people be.

When you engage and try to be right with Uncle Frank, you remove your power of influence. Uncle Frank is always going to be Uncle Frank, no matter what you tell him. If you feel your values are being violated, choose a different interaction, change the subject, or go help your mom in the kitchen. Look for the option that honors your sanity and safety. The same thing goes for Cousin Sue. You can't change her, but you can choose how much you get into her story and feed her drama.

Remember that the only thing people want in this world is to feel acknowledged and validated. But beyond that, your energy matters most. You aren't here to fix, change, or rebuild people. Rather, you're here to inspire others through your SpitFire power.

Just like a campfire, you need to create boundaries to contain and support the fire. When others around you want warmth, they'll come closer. When it's too hot for them, they'll either step away or try to put it out. Remember the Energy Boosters and Suckers.

## Dialing Your Fire Up or Down

I want you to imagine that you have a remote control for your fire dial in your pocket. As you step into each situation, environment, and interaction, you can decide whether your fire gets turned up or down. Every audience will call for a different intensity.

Imagine you're giving a presentation to a new client at work. Where do you think you should set your dial as you walk in? Ember, Flame, or Blaze? Maybe the client is very boisterous and verbose. If you're at an Ember intensity, you'll get bulldozed. If you're at a Blaze, you'll create a firestorm of competition.

Before you decide where to set your dial, observe your environment and peers. Assess the need for intensity or quiet restraint. When you know where to use your energy, you can be more efficient and effective in the long run.

## Your Self-Care Practice

We've already covered this in a previous section of The SpitFire Tetrahedron Model, but we need to drill it in. Self-Care is at the core of your ability to make anything happen on a sustainable basis, yet it's the first thing that falls off when we get "busy." Somehow, Self-Care has been misinterpreted as selfishness and self-absorption, but without it, we are ineffective at caring for others.

Think about the last time you got a good night of sleep, ate a healthy yet yummy breakfast, worked out, read, meditated, and did things on your terms. How did you feel? If you've never had a day like that, what do you think it would feel like?

Imagine that someone pulls you out of bed after four hours of sleep, demands that you serve their needs, and doesn't feed you or appreciate you. If you're a parent or caretaker, this scenario may sound familiar. But what if you're single, and you've applied this mindset to your partner, friends, or work? How can you inject Self-Care back into your routine?

Make it a priority. You aren't too busy; you just haven't made it a priority in your life. The first real step is to look in the mirror and take ownership of the fact that you've made the choice to be in this situation. So you can also make a different choice.

You don't need to wait until Monday or next month. You can start right now. You don't even need a plan; you just need to start. The plan can be shaped by forward momentum. I can't tell you how many of my clients have waited for permission to form a plan. They've had the plan and idea in them the whole time, but they lacked the confidence to take the first step.

Let's talk about your Self-Care Practice. What are three to five things you can do every day to make yourself feel awesome? I created this list of daily tasks in the Notes Application of my phone:

- Take a shower.
- Take 10,000 steps.
- Move for 30 minutes.
- Read or listen to a podcast for 30 mins.
- Meditate for at least 5 mins.
- Reach out to 2 people. Make a plan to see them, or just tell them they're awesome.

I know that when I move, learn, reach out to others, and take a shower, I feel much better than when I stay in my sweatpants all day. (This wardrobe decision-making is part of the dark side of being self-employed.) When I move and meditate, I feel a rush of creative energy and stress relief. When I learn, I stretch and grow on a new level. When I reach out to others, I expand my connected network. When I take a shower, I feel more professional and clean!

I find that my task list keeps me on point, and if I don't hit every item on that list, I don't beat myself up. I just go after it the next day. Do you need someone to be accountable to? If so, ask for help, hire a coach, or create a support network.

Think about the activities you want in your life every day. What would make you feel like a rock star? To know that you've accomplished these goals, make sure you quantify them by adding units of time or numbers of repetitions. Also make sure you connect them back to value-based intentions.

Self-Care doesn't even need to include a task list.

**Visual Reminders for Self-Care**

It could be a daily mantra, or an intention that you set for yourself every day. I've written the following three phrases on my bathroom mirror with dry-erase markers:

**Smile :)**          **Be Awesome**          **Be You**

If that isn't enough of a reminder, try something more dramatic. For example, I painted my mission statement on a canvas, which is next to my bathroom mirror:

To top it off, I have another reminder as I leave my apartment:

While these paintings don't cure my negativity, they make me smile, and help me shift out of being too serious and overthinking the things I need to let go of.

What are some quotes or messages you'd like to see every day?

_____

_____

What space do you look at every day that would be the perfect real estate for positivity? It could be your computer or your phone's wallpaper. It could be a Post-It note or magnet on your refrigerator. Wherever your eyes naturally go, give them something awesome to focus on.

# Chapter 9

## Frequently
## Asked
## Questions

Some questions came up while I was writing this book, which I thought would be helpful to share and answer.

## What Do I Do if the People Closest to Me Are Trying to Snuff Out My Flame?

This situation is super-common, and most of the time, it's completely unintentional. The people closest to us want us to be safe and unharmed. When you start straying away from the norm that your family and friends have defined for you, they may be concerned. Even when you explain your passions and desires, they may be confused or frightened about what they could mean for you (and them).

The *first step* is to understand that your fire isn't meant for everyone to understand. While your gifts may serve the masses, they aren't meant for the masses to understand. Remember when we talked about catabolic and anabolic energy? The existence of your power in an anabolic state can trigger more stress for someone in a catabolic state. The happier you get, the scarier and more detached others may feel.

The *second step* is to go back to your why. What are your intentions behind your purpose and passion? Root into them, and allow the doubt to roll past you. Collect the information you need to build your plan, but don't allow others' stories to sit with you. (In other words, don't take on other people's emotional baggage.) When you realize that their concern comes from love, you can interpret their caution as a lesson learned, and a step in a more constructive direction.

The *third step* is to let them be where they are. Most of us have the tendency to convince others that our thoughts and beliefs are right for everyone. Even if our beliefs are positive and service-based, we're in catabolic energy (judging right from wrong) when we try to convince others. If others ask you questions, only provide them with the information you're comfortable sharing, without the expectations of shifting their opinions.

Don't try to change other people. Instead, be a powerfully positive example. Then when people are ready to get onboard your happy train, you're ready for them, without judgment. This step is super-challenging, but once you can master it, you can really leverage your SpitFire Power.

## Can Introverts Be SpitFires?

Abso-freakin-lutely! To answer this question, I interviewed my friend Patricia for The SpitFire Podcast. I met her in 2015 during a coaching certification class. Most extroverts won't shut up (myself included), but Patricia is a sponge for knowledge. She's so introspective.

On the last day of our first three-day module, we shared our one-year visions. When Patricia spoke, a hush occurred that extended beyond silence. "I will be living in France, celebrating that my book was just published." Her confidence permeated the room, and we all knew she meant business.

Two years later, Patricia published a book called *Growing Bold*. She's now living in Perpignan, France, and she's working on her second book. Just because she doesn't need to be the center of the social universe, that doesn't mean she doesn't Spit Fire. Whether written or spoken, her words are thoughtful, and they mean something. When she speaks, people listen.

Her inner fire may be concealed, but it burns deeply and intensely. The more Patricia connects to others and leverages her passion and creativity, the brighter her inner fire burns.

*Update: Shortly after Patricia's appearance on The SpitFire Podcast, she took the bold step to create her own show. I got to be a guest on Discovering Courage (Episode 8) and highly recommend checking it out! www.discoveringcourage.com*

## Do I Need to Quit My Job to Be a SpitFire?

No! You do not need to quit your job to be a SpitFire. In fact, don't quit your job unless you have a sustainable, purpose-based plan. Powerhouse SpitFires act from passion and purpose, not reactive impulse. If you're itching to leave your job, a Career Coach can give you guidance and a strategy about what to do next.

Are you unsure about what to do, but know you don't like your current situation? If so, I've laid out four options in The Stay/Go Model:

## Do I Need to Be an Entrepreneur to Be a SpitFire?

No! Everyone isn't meant to be an entrepreneur, but somehow, it's become a new, sexy term. If you like your job, stay there. If you want more passion and creativity, add a project that fuels and serves you. If you want to start a business, create a plan in phases.

My story is unique to me. I was inspired to act, but I also had a financial safety net that allowed me to experiment as a business owner for one or two years. And I knew that if I didn't take a bold step, I couldn't show up as my most powerful self.

The key is understanding what your financial, emotional, and spiritual comfort levels are with risks. If you want a guaranteed paycheck, being a full-time entrepreneur probably isn't for you. If you want more of a challenge and feel confined to a desk, start a side hustle, and grow it. If you have the resources and courage to try out entrepreneurship, shadow a business owner you look up to, or work with a coach or mentor.

Whatever you decide to do, know that you don't need to do it alone. There are tons of entrepreneurial pitfalls. You can read about 13 of the ones I've pinpointed at www.spitfirecoach.com/blog/entrepreneurpitfalls.

## Do I Need to Leave My Marriage to Be a SpitFire?

No! You don't need to do anything drastic to be a SpitFire, because you've always been a SpitFire. You may be in a relationship that doesn't serve your passion. You may be projecting judgments and excuses on the other person, which are related to your own dissatisfaction.

But before you do anything hasty, sit with yourself. What do you really need that's independent of anyone else? What could you do for yourself right now that would increase your passion by a point or two? How can you make small shifts to improve your situation?

You do a lot of growth work on yourself, but the person you're in a relationship with isn't on board. What will probably happen? They'll respond by saying that's not who they met, or what they signed up for. That's okay. Sometimes, you have to let people be where they are.

Change can be really scary for the people closest to you. Be a positive example, and answer their questions without judgment or resentment. But also understand that they may not understand what's happening.

As a true SpitFire, you have the ability to light other people's fires, but only when they're ready.

## How Do You Know If You're a SpitFire?

I'm going to answer a question with some other questions: How do you know you're alive? How do you know you're happy? How do you know you're unhappy? You now have a list of your own custom SpitFire qualifications:   your passion, your energy, your motivation, your Self-Care, and your expression. Go through that list, and ask yourself how you're doing. If you're not at 100%, what could you do differently? Who could you ask for help?

## Is Everyone a SpitFire?

Yes. I believe everyone has the ability to be a SpitFire. Yes, I'm biased. I've also witnessed the shyest, most timid individuals own their power and project their own voice. Once they tap into that passion and self-worth, they're unstoppable.

All of our flames are different, but once you emerge as a SpitFire, you'll attract others who share your passion and bring support in the same way that you inspire it others.

## How Much Fire Is Too Much?

I'd say a full-size blowtorch is probably too much, but those cute little ones that make the crust on the crème brûlée are amazing!

In all seriousness, know your audience, get in touch with your intention, and gauge which setting will give you the best result. Everyone isn't ready for the Blaze, and you may singe some eyebrows. Most people are probably playing it too safe and small. So whatever you think is okay, bring another 10-20% to the party. And if you're too much, you can always dial it back. Trust yourself!

# The SpitFire Pledge

Congratulations! You've made it through *Spitting Fire*. I knew you could do it. I'd love for you to become a part of our growing community of SpitFires, but first, it's time to make your SpitFire Pledge.

If you're ready to own your title as a SpitFire, review the below pledge, or go to www.spitfirecoach.com/pledge, enter the passcode **ISPITFIRE** when prompted, and agree to the pledge below. After you fill in your details, you'll receive your customized SpitFire Certificate.

## The Pledge

I, (State Your Name), do hereby proclaim myself to be a SpitFire. As a SpitFire, I agree to:

1) Unapologetically be me.
2) Ask for help before I'm in the weeds.
3) Accept compliments.
4) Learn and grow from criticisms.
5) Support and encourage other SpitFires in the journey to awesomeness.
6) Light fires of inspiration.
7) Rest as needed.
8) Take care of myself ahead of anyone else.
9) Share my SpitFire story.

By agreeing to the above pledge, you'll receive your Certificate of SpitFire and an invitation to join the SpitFire Circle.

# Acknowledgements

To some, this book seemed to appear out of thin air. It took me about six weeks to brainstorm and write out the concepts, but if you're a writer, you know that this is where the process begins. There are multiple rounds of editing, proofreading, designing, etc. that can drive you nuts. This is where I stopped when I started writing my first book.

But this time I was determined to make this book happen. Not because I needed a glamour project, but because I needed to stop making excuses about why I hadn't written a book. In my mind the book was the key to speaking and evolving my brand as The SpitFire Coach. The idea of the book became my block to success.

The coach needed to be coached! I decided to use my own exercises and principles to break out of my limited mindset. I got back to my passion and purpose and felt a surge of power I had never felt before. I was scared, but I was ready to stop making excuses and start walking my talk.

This book has been a huge learning opportunity for me and I'm beyond proud of myself for launching beyond the status quo. But, this section isn't about me, it's about my SpitFire Circle of Support who stepped up and in to keep me on task and track.

There have been so many people who were involved in keeping my spirits up when I wanted to give up, who checked me when I wasn't being honest to my vision, and who just let me crawl into a ball when I needed to rest.

This book is for my clients who have uncovered and continue to access their SpitFire powers. Every session, email, and text are a reminder that we can always be more powerful with the right catalyst and plan.

I want to thank my friends who have supported and challenged me to be bigger than I could ever imagine, my Mom who has fostered and nurtured my unique gifts while checking my bratty stubborn side, Justin for reminding me to always focus on the "Awesome Shit", my crazy neighbors who have become my family and the random people who humored me when I was talking my way through the concepts and gave me honest feedback to make this book a true representation of what spins around in my head.

Believe it or not, I'm not good at the mushy stuff. I'll end it here by saying I love and appreciate the people in my life more than they'll ever know. I can't always verbalize my gratitude, but I hope you can see your contribution in the words, themes and stories I shared.

I'll leave it on the same note that I wrap all of the episodes of The SpitFire Podcast.

**For all the SpitFires out there, Keep Being Awesome!**

# Resources

For Business and Life Coaching from Certified Coach, Lauren LeMunyan, please visit www.spitfirecoach.com

## The SpitFire Podcast

www.spitfirepodcast.com

## The SpitFire Group Coaching Circle

www.spitfirecircle.com

## ICF (International Coach Federation)

www.coachfederation.org

## iPEC (Institute for Professional Excellence in Coaching)

www.ipeccoaching.com

26515980R00080

Made in the USA
Columbia, SC
13 September 2018